A Haverin' History of Scotland

There are few more impressive sights in the world than a Scotsman making things up.

J.M. Barrie

NORMAN FERGUSON has been writing for over fifteen years and can now do joined-up letters and everything. He started writing comedy for radio with BBC Radio 2, Radio 4, Radio Scotland and 5 Live. He has also written for TV comedy sketch shows such as Channel 4's *Smack the Pony*. His comedy claim to fame is making Radiohead's Thom Yorke laugh on Radio 1. He lives in Edinburgh.*

*Norman, not Thom Yorke.

A Haverin' History of Scotland

Norman Ferguson

Dedicated to all the people of Scotland.
Especially those who buy this book.

Cover illustrations:
Front: © Martin Latham.
Back: © Alan Rowe.

First published 2018
Reprinted 2018

The History Press
The Mill, Brimscombe Port
Stroud, Gloucestershire, GL5 2QG
www.thehistorypress.co.uk

British Library Cataloguing in Publication Data.
A catalogue record for this book is available from the British Library.

ISBN 978 0 7509 8693 9

Typesetting and origination by The History Press

CONTENTS

INTRODUCTION

Scotland is as old as any other country – maybe more so, judging by the state of the pavements. Charity shops and libraries are full of history books that give a full account of the long and winding road of Scotland's past. TC 'Top Cat' Smout, Tam 'Tom' Devine, Fiona 'Fiona' Watson – these are just some of the names that appear on the front of well-researched incisive tomes, none of which were read by this author, who gets his history from Ladybird books, the Internet and Top Trumps cards.* This lack of historical rigour and accuracy should not stand in the way of a publisher's deadline and most of the incidents and events are true(ish). As the old Scottish proverb says, 'Minesweeper doesn't play itself'.

Now history – even the well-written, exhaustively researched stuff – can tend to concentrate on the comings and goings of monarchs. The lives of the common people like you and me are often forgotten amongst tales of the kings and queens and fairy princesses who were born to

* William Wallace scores well on battles, but not so high on longevity.

rule over the common and usually dirty peasants. This is not because these common people's lives were in any way boring or uninteresting, it's just that no one wrote Ladybird books about them. Which probably does mean they were boring and uninteresting.

But as all good things have to come to an end, all bad things have to come to a start.

Let us begin at the very beginning …

1 THE BIG BANG

OR

THAT WAS LOUDER THAN THE ONE O'CLOCK GUN

There are two ways of looking at the formation of the universe. There's the 'God way', which is simple: a bearded man (or woman – hashtag Everyday Sexism Alert) issued some spells – hocus pocus, abracadabra, etc. – and lo and behold the Earth and light and stars and gravity, etc. were formed. The other, which is repeated by scientists endlessly if you get stuck at a party with them, is that there was a 'Big Bang'. This supposedly flung particles such as atoms and protons and photons and the like out into space and then some stuff happened that definitely wasn't magic but actual Proper Science. Atoms such as hydrogen and oxygen met and got on so well they joined together in what would later be called 'chemistry' and formed a 'chemical' called 'water'. This water needed a place to go and luckily such a place was being formed: Scotland.

Scotland was on a planet (glamorously named 'Earth') located in a galaxy which, appropriately for a nation of sweet-toothed inhabitants, was named after a chocolate bar: The Milky Way. The land on which the country stood was originally part of the Mediterranean coast and would have stayed there but for a dispute over image rights.

However, there were other things going on under the surface – literally. Huge things called tectonic plates move slowly – even slower than the attitudes of the West Lothian Orange Order – and it took aeons until the assorted land, lochs and bits where anthrax would be tested came to form what we would call Scotland. And what the rest of the world would call … Scotland.

The country's shape around this time was much like it is now. We all know Italy resembles a boot and Ireland resembles a koala bear. Scotland looked like many of its future inhabitants in that it had a large, wide bottom and was craggy at the top. And there is also a part that looks like a very rude part of the human anatomy, but it's best to stop right there before anyone of a sensitive disposition finds out that the Mull of Kintyre looks like a large male **[word edited out on grounds of taste]**.

Other lands were created too, of course: Iceland, due to it having a lot of ice; Greenland, as it was populated by inexperienced people, and Finland due to its large population of sharks. It would be both presumptuous and arrogant to claim that Scotland was the most beautiful of all the lands: you'd be blithely ignoring the presence of Saltcoats.*

Due to the forces of geology that lie under our feet (unless you're lying down while reading this, in which case – under your bum) the western part of Scotland is rising. Now it's not something to panic about, and it's not that you'd notice it (Scots have never been showy). At the end of the age when the land was covered with ice and when the weight of the glaciers was gone, this part of the land mass started to lift. Could it lead to all of Scotland becoming free of the ground underneath? Could the whole country float off and – powered with all those wind farms – one day fulfil the crazy dreams of

* Which most do.

many and be steered back towards its rightful place in the Mediterranean, where Scots can relax in the balmy warmth and burn those weary, winter clothes?*

Can you imagine though: Ochilview olives, Greenock grapes, Wick wines? Sound nice, don't they? Shame it'll never happen. Thanks, geology. For nothing.

BEN NEVIS

Scotland's highest point is Ben Nevis. The lowest point is that draw with Iran in the 1978 World Cup. Big Ben is the highest mountain in the whole of Britain and it sits at over 4,000ft. That's all it does. Just sits. It's a very lazy hill. It's said that for 300 days a year, fog covers its top. This is a boon for local tourism businesses as climbers don't know if they've reached the summit and so come back to make sure. As the old Scottish proverb says, 'Repeat business is good business'.

RAIN

In a recent interview, a meteorologist was asked if Scotland got more rain than the other parts of Britain. He replied, 'Yes.' He wasn't lying. It doesn't just rain in Scotland, it rrrrrrrains. If the rain in Spain stays mainly on the plain, the rain in Scotland stays mainly on everyone. As the old Scottish proverb says, 'Well, you should have brought your umbrella, shouldn't you?' So wise.

* Sadly, no.

WIND

Of course, it doesn't just rain in Scotland. It also blows. The strongest wind ever recorded was at Cairn Gorm. (Its sister hill does not have a cairn and is therefore Cairn Gormless.) The wind speed on this occasion was recorded at 172mph. If you can't imagine how fast this is, picture how quickly you can close the door, douse the lights and get hidden behind the sofa at Halloween when the hefty kids come down your street looking for sweets.

COAST

According to experts, Scotland's coast is the second most intricate in the whole world. On an episode of the television programme *We Made a Programme About the Coast*, an expert stated that due to the effect of fractals on measuring, the coastline is infinite. Eh? What have they been smoking? This 'expert' explained that if you measured the distance around a bay using a 1m ruler and it gave a distance of 200m and then you measured it with a 50cm ruler it would give a distance of 250m and if you used a 25cm ruler it would give 300m and so on and on. To *infinity*. This is not of immediate historical or comedic value, but it blew the writer of this book's tiny mind when he heard it and he thought it worth sharing. It's *infinite*? What the actual?

OLD

According to a display panel hastily scanned in a museum, Scottish rocks are amongst the oldest in the world. Take that, Bavarian gneiss! In your face, Australian breccia! Scots rocks are so old they remember when you could find a reasonably priced hotel in Edinburgh in August. Some of these rocks have become features of their own: Dumbarton Rock, Bass Rock and Edinburgh Rock – although the last one is actually sold as confectionery. Dentists in Scotland are very well off.

DINOSAURS

The early land of Scotland was inhabited by dinosaurs, one of which liked it so much she stayed around for the following millenniums. To the doubters who naysay the existence of this old creature – commonly known as 'the Loch Ness Monster'* – of course Nessie exists. She's got a page on Wikipedia. As the kids say a lot, 'Duh, Dad!'

Sadly, all the other dinosaurs succumbed to thrombosis from sitting around waiting on their paws to evolve (hello, Tyrannosaurus rex) or their necks to shorten so they could enjoy a meal the same month it was chewed (hello, those long-neckedosaurus ones). Many scientists now claim a

* Not exactly a moniker that's likely to cause the creature to want to appear publicly. Would you want to come in front of a crowd who've called you a monster? Look what happened to Frankenstein's monster ...

meteor killed the dinosaurs but, as with all things scientific, it depends on how much faith you put in the evidence.*

The dinosaurs were followed in the evolutionary track by animals such as the Smilodon, more commonly known as the sabre-toothed tiger, which the tigers themselves were well pleased with – Smilodon indeed. They got through a helluva lot of Bonjela** though – imagine biting your tongue with those colossal canines in your mouth?

Other beasts around at the time were woolly mammoths. Jumpers woven from their wool were hideously expensive, mainly due to the compensation packages paid out to wool collectors' families. The mammoths, who received nothing in the way of financial reward, did not take kindly to being sheared, especially with the Ice Age coming up.*** They thought they'd show the money-grabbing fleece-baggers who was boss and immediately made themselves extinct. Talk about cutting off your trunk to spite your face …

EARLY HUMANS

Soon it was time for the quadrupeds to move over as the bipeds were making their move. These early humans were called *Homo erectus*, which is the sort of name that puerile schoolboys would have a field day with but luckily the

* If you get this joke, well done. If not, don't worry, a scientist will explain its hilariousness to you. Stephen Hawking would have thought this a tinger.

** Other pain-relieving mouth gels are available.

*** Belated spoiler alert!

discerning readers of this tome are way above such inanity and wouldn't stand for such erectile humour dysfunction.

After a while, and bored of being in caves frightened of being eaten by a huge beast, they evolved into another species: *Homo sapiens*. This was not a great success. As the name implies, saps they were and they got sand kicked in their faces by the other bipeds that were on the scene, such as the *Homo bulliens*.

CAVE PAINTINGS

Despite the image some might have, these early humanoids weren't just hairy-arsed creatures grunting and going around scratching their hairy arses. Yes, they did do that quite a lot, but they had time (plenty of time) to do other things. One thing was art classes and now thousands of tourists, thousands of years later, go to see the astonishing images of animals, painted thousands of years ago by cave dwellers who dwelled in these caves thousands of years ago. Sadly, these thousands have to go to France as there aren't any prehistoric marvels left in Scotland's caves. They have been covered by more modern 'artwork' along the lines of sentiments such as 'Jaydyene luvs Suggsy', 'Bumby Nolan is a bum' and graphical depictions of the act of physical love. It is believed no visitor has ever come from France to see these.

2 THE ICE AGE

OR

WHEN WILL A SCOTSPERSON INVENT ANTI-FREEZE?

The Ice Age was a dramatic time of ice and snow mixed with complaints about the council's gritting services. It wasn't all icy doom and snowy gloom, however. Energy companies called it the Good Times Age, but eventually the citizens discovered they could collect their own sticks to burn and these companies became extinct.

There had been a mass migration of those who didn't like the cold much, who moved south to warmer places such as France and Spain and Anywhere But Scotland. They missed the *Sunday Post* newspaper and the couthy banter (couthy banter) and longed to return north but they couldn't. The ice had formed things called 'glaciers' – large blocks of ice that were very cold and very hard, very similar to the stare you get when you suggest spending Christmas in your own house this year. These glaciers were not too keen on the cold themselves and raced southwards to escape at a rate of 1mm per century.

Eventually the Ice Age ended (or rather, melted) as temperatures started to rise. Humans started to edge cautiously northwards. Some stopped off in what became known as 'London'. They ate cockles and mussels and sang Chas 'n' Dave ditties to keep warm. They had no idea what a 'Snooker Loopy' was, but they were simple folk and it didn't keep them awake at night. What did was anxiety. They were anxious, worried about what lay north of Watford, but the brave souls amongst them continued, searching onwards, venturing forwards through the rugged terrain until they reached the wild, untamed lands of Luton and Stevenage. Those who had taken utter leave of their senses carried on further (farther?)* north. After much walking, they reached the place we call Scotland. They took one look and turned straight round until someone pointed out that summer was drawing near and they'd need to find warm shelter. So, they carried on.

EARLY PEOPLES

These early peoples could be described as 'nomads' but many called them 'Very Much Mads' in the punning jocularity that, along with most people of the time, soon died out. Life was hard. And short. There were many things that could kill you. The stress of not knowing anything about mindfulness and how to cope with anxiety was chief amongst the killers.

It was a shame these early peoples couldn't enjoy their environment. They found an abundance of foodstuffs: ripe berries, succulent game birds, tender mammals, tasty sea fish – all of which they made even more delicious by frying in golden batter and burying in salt. There was plenty of food to go around as the population of Scotland around this time was about 10,000. The population was so small they all knew each other by name. Ug, Ugg and Uggg were popular names, but it could lead to confusion over spellings, so eventually they all decided to call themselves Shug.

However, with such a small population there was nothing that everyone didn't know. Go around with your

* We'll catch this in the edit.

mammoth pants on outside-in and the whole country was laughing at you, Mr Silly Outside-In Mammoth Pants. This resulted in what was later known as introspection, without which much poetry and indie music might never have happened.

These early humans became hunter-gatherers. The men-humans gathered to talk about that *really* big one they almost caught and the women sat around raising the children, making the food, cleaning the fur coats, arranging the babysitting rota, washing the area behind children's ears, hoping a Scotsperson would invent scissors soon so they'd be able to tell their children not to run with them, rearranging the stone furniture and so on, and if there was time they'd bake, mend the tablecloths, plan social gatherings, go over the homework, fantasise about a time when those do-nothing menfolk would put up a rock shelf without having to be awarded a medal for it, and so on.

These hunter-gatherers used tools known as microliths (small, flinty cutting tools made from stone) that are easily confused with microlights (small, flimsy aircraft used to cut down the numbers of amateur pilots). These tools were colour-coded for health and safety hygiene reasons:

Green – poultry
Red – fish
Blue – vegetables
Yellow – sacrificing family members.

Yes, life was hard but it was organic, which counts for something. And in this hippy paradise there was an abundance of wild herbs, spices and – unfortunately for those entranced by beauty who were enjoying being in the moment (and not keeping a good lookout) – sudden death by predator. It was something else to get stressed about.

FIRE

Around this time there was one major element missing from life: fire, without which lighting cigarettes was impossible. Once fire was invented (by a Scotsperson, despite Scotland not having been officially invented yet – that's how innovative Scots are), life was transformed for these primitive and hairy creatures. With fire came light and they could now see what utter squalor they were living in: the window sills were inches deep in dust, there were bones lying about, and as for the toilets, well it's something to be thankful for that the sense of smell hadn't evolved too much.

With their caves now lit in the long, dark evenings, these early Scots-to-be could now have friends over for dinner and entertain into the night and, more lethally, forget about the boiling-over chip pans and then asphyxiate themselves when they fell asleep. Although fire had been invented, fire brigades hadn't.

3 THE STONE AGE

OR

WHEN WILL PLASTIC BAGS BE INVENTED?

These early peoples in early Scotland lived in a world very different to ours. They had to get through life without BBC's *Reporting Scotland*. It's impossible to comprehend life like that. If a cat was stuck up a tree in Peebles they didn't get to hear about it for *weeks*. But this wasn't all – they had no central heating, no medicine and no fleece jumpers, although they could use animal hides for warmth. Most of the animals didn't mind too much, as long as they were still inside their hides when involved. When they discovered there was a fondness for their skins *without* themselves attached they felt less happy, and invented a popular Scottish pastime: being miserable.

The people of this time are sometimes called the Late Neoliths. This really annoyed the Early Neoliths who couldn't see what was so hard about turning up on time. But the Late Neoliths were there in time for their own period, so it worked out okay. Eventually they died and doubly justified their label.

SKARA BRAE

One of the most remote habitats – unless you were there already – was at Skara Brae (Skara Brae) in Orkney. The Braerarians had a lovely spot near the beach, handily close to the Historic Scotland visitor centre. This, however, proved to be detrimental to their well-being, with many succumbing to diabetes from overindulgence on chocolate chip shortbread. This led to another round of gleeful hand rubbing by Scottish dentists.

As this was the Stone Age, the dwelling places were built of stone and boy were they long-lasting. They had to be. They were inhabited for 600 years – that's how long it took to pay off the mortgage. The old Scots proverb might say, 'Where there's muck, there's brass', but it could also say, 'Where there's stone, there's money'.

Skara Brae was a prime site, much in demand. These compact and bijou residences, with open sea views and easy access to amenities (the dung heap was out the back), afforded good protection against invaders and carnivores. It was these qualities and more that later attracted Mary, Queen of Scots to stay there in an attempt to avoid being shouted at by John Knox.

BEAKER PEOPLE

You hope, when you leave this life behind, that you will leave some remnant, some mark that says, 'I was here'. It's a natural urge to feel our time on the planet was not just a temporary sojourn from which we depart without a trace. Who wants to feel the way Willie Rennie* will feel when he leaves political office?

One group who left a mark, of sorts, were the Beaker People. You will not guess what they left behind. Go on. Beakers? Yes! It's not stupendous is it? Beakers are great, don't get me wrong – they hold liquid and you can pour liquids out of them into other containers which may or

* A Scottish politician from the er ... the erm ... um, one of the parties in Scotland.

may not be beakers, but as a legacy of a people it's not in the top rank. Will citizens of the 1970s be known as the Tupperware People? It should cause citizens to ponder what they will be remembered for down the centuries. Are we the Dog Ball Chucker Folk?

STONED CIRCLES

Around this time stone circles began to appear on the landscape. The meaning of them is still unclear. Were they sacrificial sites? Sites of religious worship? Early skateboard parks? We just don't know. Having said that, the writer of this book doesn't know what that silver trumpet beside the M8 motorway between Glasgow and Edinburgh signifies, and he lives there now.*

FARMING

In human history there are few leaps of human advancement equal to farming, although screw-top wine bottles come a close second. With farming, communities and families were able to settle down and channel their energies into working a distinct piece of land. And moaning about Europe.

It wasn't supremely successful at first. The early farmers faced huge challenges, chief of which being – they didn't know how to farm. There were no agricultural colleges

* And has trouble getting to sleep. Those trucks are noisy!

and no countryside TV programmes and so they resorted to trial and error. Farmers and their families would approach starvation as they waited to see if a crop would come up out of the ground. One of the hurdles they faced was, in their innocent country state of knowing nothing, they'd planted stone pebbles instead of seeds. They would then eat the pebbles in desperation, helping along that thriving industry of dentistry.

Around this time tools were not fully developed. Things like ploughs, scythes and those things that whirl round and thresh things hadn't been invented by Scotspersons yet. But those in farming were determined and adopted rituals that became traditions, such as getting up in the dark, working all hours and getting covered in cow s★★t. Though this sounded good in itself, many longed for the lost days of hunting and gathering when they could gather and hunt without fear of being caught using the wrong-coloured diesel in their cars by those b★★★★★s from Europe.

Soon however, farming went from strength to strength and new words entered the Scottish language: neeps, sheuch, byres, dreels, sharn, kye, tumshie, numptie. These great words were adopted by all working on the land, even though they had no idea what they meant.

Animals were looked after in a practice known as 'animal husbandry', which was too wide a term as very few farmers ever married their beasts. Pigs, goats, sheep, cows and bears* were kept for their milk, eggs and waterproof coverings. Just as they had tried to farm the

* Not for long.

land without knowing what to do, these country folks' attempts at harvesting eggs from cows and leather from chickens proved to be mostly unsuccessful.

But work wasn't enough and some farmers soon got lonely living in the countryside and went off to form villages. These village people created a rudimentary language and communicated by forming letter shapes in the air with their hands and arms. This led to 'disco dancing', which was viewed with alarm by Calvinists worried people would start enjoying themselves.

Peoples from the villages (townies) mixed with those from the country (bumpkins) and they would talk about common matters: how things were better 'back then' even though 'back then' was last Tuesday and how awful disco dancing was.

DEATH

These early Scottish residents were very keen on death. Not the actual dying – the only people keen on that are kamikaze pilots or those who bought season tickets when Berti Vogts was Scotland's football manager – but the commemoration of those recently departed. Tombs were all the rage. Best Tomb of the Year was a highly sought-after prize – to the point of violence. If a village had no recent deaths, and therefore no tombs, the organising committee would look around for a suitable volunteer and smooth their passage into the hereafter. It was seen as a great honour to be sacrificed for the glory of the local community. (Education wasn't really a thing back then.) Tombs would be built to align with celestial events, whether they be the Winter Solstice or the Summer Solstice. Autumn and spring didn't get a solstice as they wouldn't tidy up after dinner.

Those able to build these stone memorials to the recently departed became a valuable part of the social infrastructure and gained a special identity. The men who built a big tomb on Orkney called Maes Howe (Maes Howe) saw the name stick: maesons.

4 THE BRONZE AGE

OR

ANY SIGN OF PLASTIC BEING INVENTED?

The Bronze Age is noted for the preponderance of things made of gold – no, wait, it was bronze. Things like brooches, rings, medallions, weapons, furniture, bras, children's toys, washing machines and so on.

Bronze jewellery was all the rage. Before, people had used their fingers to pick up food or pick their noses, but now they discovered they could encircle them in bits of shiny metal. And if they put a 'special ring' on a 'special finger' of a special person they got to do 'special things'* with them in the privacy of their dwellings. This made bronze very, very popular.

Another of the by-products of the bronze bling being produced was it marked out the class system. The well-heeled were able to show their wealth through ostentatious displays of expensive jewellery. The Fur-Coat-No-Knickers** Brigade had arrived in force. They also demanded the poor be packed off to the underworld away from their own grand tombs. They didn't want to be seen dead with the lower-class corpses.

HOUSES

Architecture developed, although no one called it that as a Scotsperson hadn't invented Latin yet. Different buildings were devised, so circular constructions were called roundhouses, places shaped like wheels were named

* Sex.

** They hadn't been invented yet.

wheelhouses and places to go to the toilet were also built. Showing the inventiveness that came to be known around the world, these early Scotspersons built crannogs (crannogs) which were houses on stilts (stilts), plonked in the middle of lochs (lochs). Apart from the excellent security aspects (any burglar would have to own a canoe and a ladder, which is the stuff of dreams for *You've Been Framed* viewers), having a toilet 20ft above a large expanse of water certainly took care of any sewerage disposal issues, although the indigenous Brown-Headed Swans eventually took umbrage. And flight.

FOOD

Those living around these times were healthier than many of us living today, despite our probiotic yogurts and direct-debited gym memberships. Recent studies of their poo* show they ate a good diet of nuts, seafood, berries and meats such as lamb and venison. (Of course, it wasn't *that* good a diet as they're all dead now.) These foodstuffs are still available, but at farmers' markets at prices that would make a Bronze Age person laugh until they weed into their fur pants.

With so many things being made from bronze, it came as no surprise when it eventually ran out and the Age ended, just in time, for another Age.

* It's a crap job but someone has to do it. Someone who wasn't paying enough attention in their school's career sessions.

5 THE IRON AGE

OR

SERIOUSLY, NO PLASTIC YET?

The Iron Age saw people sporting clothes free of creases that made them far more successful at job interviews. The material used to make their 'irons' caught on and soon anything and everything was made with this new wonder material that wasn't stinky old bronze: leg irons, grid irons (no idea), golf irons and other items you could leave in a fire to show how busy you were. They weren't finished with this list – oh no. They made big things, things that would move. If pulled by horses,* that is.

Some of these horses weren't keen and had to be encouraged, hence the Scottish invention of sugar lumps which was much applauded by veterinary dentists. These newfangled wheeled vehicles, or 'chariots', were later made famous by Charlton Heston in the biblical movie *Chariots of Fire*. Interestingly, in Twenty Oatcake a chariot was found in Edinburgh where it had lain undisturbed for centuries, ever since getting its wheel stuck in a tramline.

There was one issue with this wonder product. Much time was spent telling each other off for pronouncing it 'irn' and not 'eye-ron' as the posher speakers preferred. Unfortunately, this could degenerate into physical use of items made of irn and eye-ron on each other's skulls.

* The horses were made of flesh and bones and some squidgy stuff.

SECURITY

Around this time people fell out over other issues, not just pronunciation. You see, they hadn't had any Christianity yet so there was a great deal of coveting asses, coveting oxen and anything else going. Sometimes this coveting could get a bit rowdy so measures were taken to protect properties. Children were sent up trees on guard duty with megaphones made from mammoth tusks to yell, 'Stranger! We're in danger!' and 'No, we don't want our driveway cleaned thanks!'

While not without merit, it wasn't enough to stop a reasonably determined marauder carrying jaggy things made of iron, so some fortification was desired. Hill forts were built, but not everyone had a hill nearby. If they tried to get onto a hill those in the hill forts told them to fort off, so they went home and had a bit of a cry. Then they came up with an idea – build their own hills! But they didn't have enough earth and if they dug it out of the ground they ended up building their own pits. So, they came up with the idea of 'brochs'. People wetted their fur pants laughing. You couldn't live in a piece of jewellery, they said, through great gulps of gasping for air. They're too small!

The maesons shook their heads, cursing their luck for living in an age of poor hearing. When they explained they weren't 'brooches' but stone towers called 'brochs' everyone saw the funny side. Some of these stone dwelling places are still standing and people are still inside them wishing they hadn't laughed so much at the maesons.

DECORATION

One of the features of houses of the time, which may appear unusual to modern peoples, was the adorning of dwelling paces with the lopped-off heads of opponents. It was supposed to bring good luck, but one thing it didn't bring was visitors. It was bad enough being worried about spilling wine on your neighbour's new carpet without being concerned you were going to have your noggin severed and stuck above the fireplace. Luckily, fashion moved on and walls were covered with the corpses of ducks flying in a row.

Unfortunately for many of the created objects of the time, the weather had a role to play and the Iron Age was soon followed by another period.

THE RUST AGE

There are some who claim that the amount of rust around fed into human DNA chains and led to what is known as 'ginger hair', but nothing too scientific can back this up, which is a shame as people could say they really were built from girders.

BOREDOM

Throughout the prehistoric times, many of the early peoples were bored. Their pastoral existence was all fine and dandy but they yearned for some glamour and excitement. Years would pass as they idled away their time plaiting hair, applying woad and inventing iron things. Let's face it, you'd be bored out of your skull too – there was nothing to Instagram with! It took a while, but in the First Century Oatcake AD all the excitement they could hope for came with the arrival of a people for whom taking Latin was not a boring options course but a language.

6 THE ROMANS

OR

DUDE, WHERE'S MY CHARIOT?

The Romans bestrode Europe like all-conquering conquerors because that's what they were. They were also exotic and charming, well, when they weren't trying to drag you off to be a slave or stabbing you with their pointy swords or making you learn Latin. The Romans called Scotland 'Caledonia', after the song by Dougie MacLean which they would oftentimes pass the hours by humming. They came, they saw, they hummed.

TRIBES

The Romans were big on keeping tabs on everyone and then writing things down. In Scotland, they noted down the following tribes:

Damnonii
Daanii
Daaniiminogue
Smertae
Notsosmertae
Cornavi
Corarmi
Coraeroplanesnotinventedbya Scotspersonyet
Venicones
Icecreamcones
Trafficcones
And others that were not as punnable.

One of the Roman chiefs was called Agricola, father to a murdered wife, brother to the equally refreshing

Pepsicola.* He oversaw the building of a huge barracks at Perth, which at the time sat on the River Tay, and still does. While there, the Roman centurions co-ordinated their military strategy while discussing at length the correct pronunciation of nearby Scone. Was it Scone? Or Scone?

HADRIAN'S WALL

The Romans built two walls in or near to Scotland. One was called Hadrian's Wall and the other wasn't. Hadrian's took seven years to build. Shows you what can be done if you have the right project management in place, dedicated staff and thousands of slaves being whipped into doing unpaid overtime. Hadrian wasn't hugely efficient, he just couldn't decide on sandstone or granite, and so much of this time was taken up with stone maesons scratching their chins, shrugging and asking if there was any chance of a biscuit with their cup of vino veritas.

ANOTHER WALL

Not happy with the first wall, the Romans had another one made. Due to budget squeezes, however, it was made of dirt. People waxed nostalgically about the old wall, how they built proper ones back then, not like these modern, rubbish ones made of dirt. However, the Antonine Wall kept people in Bo'ness away from those in Linlithgow and became much loved as a result.

* Other types of fizzy cola are available.

CULTURE

The Romans had their own song called 'Romans in the Gloaming'* which is still sung to this day, although not by Romans as they are pretty much all dead. This is one of the sad parts of history – most of the participants are deceased. It's not sad for publishers' lawyers, however, who know the meaning of '*La morticus est nominus litiganus*' ('the dead don't sue').

The Romans weren't, of course, all from Rome, despite their name. There were French Romans, Dutch Romans, Hungarian Romans and Romanian Romans. It was a bit like calling Prestwick Airport 'Glasgow Prestwick Airport', even though it's nowhere near Glasgow. But anyway, back to the Romans Who Weren't. This ethnic mix ticked a number of HR boxes and diversity awards were won as a result. Anyone could be dragooned into service in the Roman Army and killed, they did not discriminate. That counts for something, surely? No? Fair enough.

A FAMOUS BATTLE

The Romans won a famous battle at Mons Graupius (Mons Graupius), so famous no one knows where it took place. It's possible that the information board blew off in the wind and this historic Scottish location was lost forever, unable to echo down the centuries. It is also understandable if no one wanted to celebrate it too wildly as the local side got a horrible doing. Some estimates claim that 10,000 died.

* Gloaming – a Scottish word that means 'gloaming'.

That's a lot of people, or what an undertaker calls: a holiday home in Barbados.

The anti-Romans were led by a man called Calgacus, who later invented a maths-based torture mechanism for school children. He said about the Romans, 'They make a desert and call it peace.' His words echoed down the centuries, alongside people furrowing their foreheads and muttering, 'What the hell's he talking about? Scotland doesn't have any deserts. *Desserts* yes, but not deserts.'

After the battle, the Celts* made sure the Romans weren't getting their hands on their homes, wives, cattle or *Sunday Posts* and burnt them. They also went 'Na na na na na! You're not getting our stuff!', and did that thing where you waggle your fingers beside your ears while sticking your tongue out and wiggling it from side to side. Seeing this, the Romans edged away carefully. There were plenty more cows in the fields to fry and they could get a *Sunday Post* from the newsagent, it was no biggie.

One of the Roman legions set off on a long walk, or 'patrol' as military types like to describe them. This Ninth Legion were never seen again and despite a Hollywood film crew being with them, what happened remains one of Scotland's great mysteries, along with why was BBC Scotland's 'comedy' panel game *Caledonia MacBrayne* commissioned and how did Chris Iwelumo miss that sitter against Norway? We will never know the fate of those centurions, although 2,000 years later it's safe to assume they're not holed up in a cave playing Snap.

* More on them later.

The Romans who weren't lost eventually tired of the cold and wet environment – plus they could not get decent parmesan for love nor denari – and they left. They weren't overly enamoured of the Route One style of the local football teams, for that matter, either. Their legacy is not so easy to spot in Scotland as in other countries. There aren't many spas around and crucially there certainly aren't many straight roads. There are men who go about in bare legs and short skirts causing mayhem, though, so their legacy isn't completely gone. Who knew Romans invented stag nights?

7 THE DARK AGES

OR

HAS A SCOTSPERSON NOT INVENTED LIGHT BULBS YET?

After the Romans exeunt stage left, there was a long period called the Dark Ages. Why so called? They took all the light bulbs when they moved out. How rude is that? The words mostly heard during this period were 'Sorry, mate', 'Oops, sorry madam, I thought that was your elbow' and 'Ouch', as people bumped around in the dark. Times were hard, especially if you walked toe first into a chair leg in the middle of the night.

Eventually someone invented candles,* though when they looked around and noticed the pestilence, filth, muck and general unseemliness of how they lived they quickly blew them out.

TOWNS

Around this time there were no towns in Scotland. There were some in Europe but, as someone had had the cheek to invent them before a Scotsperson had the chance, the Scots took the huff and didn't want them. This huffiness was a trait that saw Scots refuse to take part in newfangled things such as windows, plumbing and sobriety.

Houses, like their inhabitants, always smelt of damp. It's not surprising: these dwelling places were built of mud, turf and a unique construction method called wattle and daub, which was a mixture of twigs and clay. This is a combination rarely seen on *Grand Designs*, for very good reasons. It's rubbish. Unsurprisingly, the residents weren't in love with being wet all the time in homes with the

* A Scotsperson of course.

rain resistance of a paper tissue. Luckily, with the perpetual darkness of the time they were unable to see how frizzy their hair had gone.

FOOD

Around this time, one of the great Scottish food staples was introduced: porridge. Oats, soaked in water then heated up in a pot, were to be what jellied eels were to Cockneys – something that didn't look that appetising but through tradition and custom were forced on kids on pain of not getting to watch *Peppa Pig*.

For those who really did not want to enjoy life, porridge was made with water and served with salt. Only later did people wise up and realise this was vile, and they replaced the water with milk, the salt with sugar and then added honey, before tipping it into a bin and heating up some Pop Tarts.

KING ARTHUR

There are some who believe legendary King Arthur lived in Scotland. There is some evidence to back this theory: in Edinburgh there is a large hill called Arthur's Seat and just over the Firth of Forth in Fife there is a place called Kingskettle, strongly supporting the idea that he had a cup of tea there. When you add this all up, you quickly come to the realisation that he didn't live in Edinburgh and this myth was probably made up by the early tourist boards, along with the notion of a midge-free summer.

THE PICTS, ETC.

Scotland around this time was inhabited by many groups: the Picts, Shovels, Angles, Tri-Angles, Try To See It From My Angles, Celts, Gers, Maentae* and some that history has forgotten.** Now, the writer of this book is not a linguistic expert (you've probably guessed this already), but suffice it to say that there is a wide-ranging and essentially boring debate about the languages that were spoken around this time. The main thing to remember is that those of the time were careful to mind their P-Celtics and Q-Celtics*** so as not to offend.

Of all the above groups, the Picts are the most mysterious of all. They left nothing written down. No language is known, no graffiti remains. Who were they? What were they? Which were they? They did leave things for us to ponder at in glass cases in museums; things like jewellery, stonework and stuff like that. However, some of these are not fully of the Picts – they're just Pictish.

Another of the tribes were the Scots, who were Irish. They came over the Irish Sea from Ireland to take part in what would become a traditional Scottish pastime: fighting. Firstly, against the Romans and then against the Picts who had previously been their allies. Braw.

* Named because of their fresh breath.

** They should have hired better PR agencies.

*** Nice linguistic joke there for the academics, although it's doubtful they'd risk their careers being caught reading this.

Around this time there were kings who ruled over an area of Scotland called Dal Riata (Dal Riata). In order to become king, you had to put your foot into a hole in the rock. No, really. It was the stone equivalent of Cinderella. The hole is still there, but if your foot does fit it doesn't automatically make you a monarch, despite thousands doing this every year. (What an idiot the writer of this book felt issuing edicts and installing new taxes only to be told, 'Don't be such a numptie', by the Dal Riata Council of Denying Rightful Kingships.) To become king these days you have to be born into a royal family. Although the present-day queen's husband does have a habit of 'putting his foot in it'!

Eventually the Scots of Dal Riata took over Pictish territory around Eight Hundred Oatcake. Over in another bit of the country, in the area known as Strathclyde (Strathclyde), the Britons ruled, with their HQ at a place called Alt Clut. Their previous base had been abandoned and shut down. This was a place called Ctrl Alt Del.*

But around this time, someone very important was due to turn up and be in the book.

ST COLUMBA, GOD AND BIBLES

One of the most influential figures in Scottish history is Saint Columba. With a name like that you could only be one thing – holy – and Columba was that in spades.

* *A nice joke for Microsoft Windows users.*

Born in Donegal in Ireland (which keen-eyed readers will notice is not in Scotland), he studied the Bible until he could name all the ~~dwarves~~ apostles, without hesitating over the tricky last one. He wanted to tell everyone else about this, and would stand on street corners handing out leaflets and shouting about how great God was. Irish punters couldn't get going for him jumping out in front and expounding on how great He really was. Eventually they took note and acted. And chucked him out of the country.

With Scotland just being over the water, that's where he headed. In Five Hundred Oatcake he came ashore at Iona with twelve followers, or 'stalkers' as we now call them. Columba was on a mission. He was determined to convert the Picts to believing in God and the Bible and all of that, so he set off on an epic quest with a simple message: join the Church or you'll be in for it from the Big Man upstairs.*

Was he joking? Did he have inside knowledge? Nobody was sure if they should laugh at him or immediately convert in case he was not talking a load of bullocks. After a miracle near Inverness when Columba made the doors of a castle fly open after flicking the vees at them, the leader of the Picts, King Brude, decided to convert to Christianity. Just like that, as a later magician would say. A lesson for those guys that turn up to your door wanting to clean the moss from your driveway or convert your kitchen into a conservatory. A little bit of magic action will seal the deal.

* *God.*

Columba continued his work that would echo down the centuries, going around the country like a charity fundraiser selling raffle tickets. The prizes for these winners were: a tin of biscuits, a bottle of sherry and everlasting life in Heaven. Understandably, many quite fancied the thought of that everlasting life and soon signed up. Let's face it, any sort of afterlife was better than the presentlife, scrabbling about in the filth that typified the existence of the many in those dim and distant non-shower-gel days.

The afterlife was not that far away for these peoples. The stress of eking out a living was having a bad effect on their longevity. Not only that, but cholesterol testing had not been invented by a Scotsperson yet and with the worrying, and the effect of all that red meat, many just keeled over clutching their chests and wondering where that invisible spear had come from.

The new believers went for it like ducks to holy water. Remember those beads everyone put on their car seats? Thunderbirds' Tracy Island? Men waxing their beards? Christianity was like that, but with less itching. Crosses started appearing everywhere and were soon the loom bands* of their day.

Some, however, were not convinced. These unbelievers had to be persuaded that it really was the best option for bringing peace and love – and other hippy buzzwords – to all mankind. Axes, swords and staves had, at times, to be used but the message, like those knocked unconscious and who fell into the bogs, eventually sunk in.

* Or any other fad. What exactly is a 'gluten'?

What made it easier for the Word of God (technically incorrect as there were many Words) was that only Those in the Know could Read the Words. Now it wasn't like they were making stuff up and they could tell any tall tale they liked and get away with it, it was just that not everyone could understand, let alone write, Latin. So actually they pretty much could say anything they fancied.

The Church's place in history was going to be assured. It helped that the churchmen got to write the history books. They also wrote out the Bibles, which were beautiful things: leather bound, fully illustrated, unexpurgated and only available in a limited edition, although none came signed by the author.

The uneducated stood in mesmerisation at such things. They hadn't seen many books before and this one had pictures! Some of the adventurous held them upside down to see if they'd open at the saucy bits, but they ended up with disappointment and strained elbow joints – these books were heavy. And there weren't any saucy bits. With their strong moral messages, they set the way for later picture books like *The Gruffalo* and *Elmer's Special Day*.

These Bibles were kept in 'churches', which to a younger audience are now known as 'apartments'. Cold and draughty buildings made of stone that allow no heat to linger, they fully adhere to the 11th (Scottish) Commandment: Thou Art Not Here to Enjoy Oneself.

MORE FIGHTING

Around this time (Seventh Century Oatcake) there was some more fighting, this time with tribes in England, known as the Anglo-Saxons of Northumbria, as this pretty much summed them up. The Northumbrians were able to move on up north and take territory that included Edinburgh. This upset the Edinburghians a lot, as they had nothing in the pantry and had assumed the invading hordes would have had something to eat before arriving. This led to the famous Edinburghian greeting, 'You'll have had your victuals'.

These Northumbrians under their King Ecgfrith had designs on other parts of Scotland and this led to, guess what? Yes, a battle! The Battle of Nechtansmere, which took place near a place called Forfar* in Angus. This is the town where the locals bemoan not being far enough away from Dundee.** The battle saw many dead and the injured would lie on the ground moaning and groaning until they died or got better. But it didn't matter, as the Picts had won! King Eggwhisk's troops had been royally defeated by King Brude, who has already appeared in this book and who would later make his mark on history by also appearing in the next section.

* One of the places where Mary, Queen of Scots stayed in an attempt to avoid being shouted at by John Knox.

** And the vice is versa.

KING KENNY

King Kenneth McAlpin was a king and notable for being the first king to unite all of Scotland.* That's what kings in them days did. Thanks, Kenneth. His name is subject to much misinterpretation by cloth ears, who thought he was Kenneth Make Alpen, a breakfast dish of nuts, dried fruit and other bits and bobs. Others got it completely round their necks and thought he was Kenneth MacAlpine, after the area of mountainous Europe known for skiing. A move from the people of Appin to have him as one of their own failed, but it was worth a try.

Whatever his surname, this King Kenny was a goodly monarch, well loved by all his subjects and whose exploits would echo down the centuries. Kenny did his 'kingly duties' in the bedroom area, and with the help of his wife produced sons and daughters. His two sons, Constantine and Aed, went on to become monarchs themselves, although the latter was not hugely appreciated by his subjects as no one knew how to pronounce his name.

* Some 'historians' with PhDs and the like have claimed he wasn't, but it suits no one to get bogged down in 'detail' or 'facts' this close to a publisher's deadline.

VIKINGS

Vikings are amongst those peoples who have had a bad press, and there's no way this is going to stop now. One of the chief complaints raised by Vikingophiles is that the Norsemen never wore those horned hats. They're not too bothered by the allegations about the pillaging, raping, burning, looting and so on, but lay off the pointy hats that weren't pointy and that they didn't wear. People find the strangest things to get het up about. (Having said that, what is it with travel guides that list 'best undiscovered tranquil locations' in newspapers read by millions? How are they going to remain tranquil if you tell everyone about them?)

Sooooo, getting back on topic. The Vikings were renowned for sailing round Scotland looking for choice pieces of land on which to land before making off with all the shiny trinkets and fancy goods they fancied. In doing so, they started the industry that is now known as 'cruise ships'.

The Vikings loved their boats. For them it was boats, boats, boats, boats, boats, boats. And boats. They were born in boats, sailed in boats, lived in boats, did numbers one and two in boats, carried their booty home in boats and when they retired they got boat-shaped clocks. And when they died? They were cremated. In boats. In Valhalla, we can only speculate, but it's fairly likely they sit on boat-shaped clouds and talk for eternity about boats. Recent research has claimed their image of ransacking renegades is, in fact, unfair and they were mostly farmers. How do you get a tractor in a boat?

The Vikings' contribution to the world was sure to echo down the centuries. Apart from their boaty exploits, they also gave us words. One of their rulers was King Haakon, who gave his name to a type of cough. Other contributions include:

'dale' which means 'valley'
'wick' which means 'bay'
'voe' which means 'sheltered harbour'
'Viking' which means 'Viking'.

These 'Norsemen' also gave the English language the word 'Norman', meaning 'wise and effortlessly funny man of letters' which remains true to this day.

In One Thousand Oatcake, a treaty was agreed between Viking King Magnus Barelegs and Scots King Edgar Fully Troused whereby the Outer Hebrides remained part of Norway, except on Sundays when they were closed.

These Vikings had their own gods: Thor, Odin, Hulk, Wolverine, but not Iron Man – he was a Baptist. They (the Vikings, not the Baptists) were terrific sailors able to navigate their way from Scandinavia to exotic locations such as America, Italy and Ayrshire. In Twelve Sixty Oatcake, at the pretty seaside village of Largs, the Vikings came off second best in a battle with the locals. A result that many over the centuries have also experienced, especially on Bank Holiday weekends.

THE SALTIRE

Scotland's flag is a white cross on a light blue background. Or four blue triangles on a white background. It's really up to you how you view things. This flag is known as 'the Saltire'. According to legend, or as we now term it 'Wikipedia', the saltire was first seen at the battle at Athelstaneford, pronounced by the locals 'Ashenford'. (For other strange Scottish pronunciations, see Kilconquhar pronounced 'Kinnochurt', Gullane pronounced 'Gillan' and Saltcoats pronounced 'Here be dragons'.)

The battle was between the Picts of King Angus McFergus, who took on King Athelstane's Northumbrians. One of the Picts had been accused of looking at King Athelstane's girlfriend and so the battle was set up to take place 'outside'. Always up for a rumble, the Scots jumped in on the Picts' side.

During the fighting, a white cross was seen in the light blue sky and taken as a sign that they must do the Lottery that night. Some have suggested that the white cross in the sky was caused by the CIA laying chemtrails to subdue the population, but this was silly as a Scotsperson hadn't invented aircraft, the CIA, or chemtrails by then.

8 THE MIDDLE AGES

OR

NOW THAT'S WHAT I CALL A GROSS DEATH, VOLUME 27

At the start of the Middle Ages some people felt they'd missed out, not having seen the Starting Ages, although they didn't have to worry for too long as they were killed by The Plague,* or its more jocular title, The Black Death. The Plague was different from other pestilences as it was always in capital letters. The cold, the flu, the skitters – none of them got their own initial caps like The Plague did. Sufferers grew boils, they sweated all the time and smelt funny. Normal speech was replaced by a low mumbling. Had everyone become a teenager? The end, when it came, was a relief. No one wanted to have to look at these lump-ridden stinkers any longer than they had to.

THE NORMANS

Any book on Scotland has to have the Normans in it. (This tome has one on the front, too.) Coming from Normandy, the Normans had invaded England in Ten Sixty Oatcake when one of their archers had shot English King Harold in the eye with an arrow, thus winning himself a speedboat. These Normans liked what they saw and stayed.

Their influence spread north, but as they had terrible memories they insisted on writing everything down in

* Not The Plaque, that is something that happens to your teeth, but as hardly anyone had any teeth left this was never really a problem. The Middle Ages were hard on dentists.

case they forgot where they'd been.* One of the books the Normans created was called the *Domesday Book*, which recorded the number of bald-headed men in the country. Sadly, lost to history are the *Tomesday Book* (list of books) and the *Gnomesday Book* (garden ornaments).

MACBETH

Around this time there were a succession of Scottish kings with names like Donald, Duncan, Malcolm, Kenneth, and other names that would echo down the centuries. One name that would really ECHO-OO-oo-oo-oo down the centuries was Hamish Macbeth, known to superstitious actory types as 'Macbeth'.

King Macbeth was different from the one in the play by Shakespeare, in that he was a real person and not one played by actors. He was known as the Mormaer** of Moray and his wife was the poetically named Gruoch, which is that noise you make when clearing your throat before making a speech. They had a dog called Spot, whose expulsion after one too many poops on the carpet did end up in the play. Macbeth lived in a castle, which was one of the places where Mary, Queen of Scots stayed in an attempt to avoid being shouted at by John Knox.

One of the Malcolms around this time was Malcolm Three. He was known as 'Big Head', but not to his face.

* Or, in the case of Grimsby, where they hoped to forget where they'd been.

** No idea.

To his face he was known as King Malcolm. He quite fancied being king of bits of England and so started some fighting between Scotland and England. As was oftentimes the case, it wasn't a great success and in Ten Ninety Oatcake the Norman king, King William 'The Conqueror' the Conqueror, rode north up a path that would be beaten a lot (like the Scots) by English monarchs. King Willy made Malky pay homage to him, which in those days was over £100. But Malky wasn't put off the old fighting. He was spoiling for more battling and he soon got his (death) wish. In Ten Ninety Oatcake, old Big Head was gone, gone, gone after losing a battle at Alnwick.

ST MARGARET

Before he died, King Malcolm Three was married. His wife was called Queen Margaret, and Margaret and Malky had eight children together, most of whose names he could remember. Margaret was one of those people that make everyone look bad. She prayed, gave money to the poor, gave food to the poor, took their pit bulls for walkies, paid for a ferry so the poor could travel to St Andrews to pray, that sort of stuff. She was good, was good Queen Margaret. In Twelve Fifty Oatcake she was canonised. Sadly, this does not mean she was fired out of an artillery piece but was instead made a saint. It was a nice thought, but the trouble with sainthoods is you only get them when you're dead, a bit like that bit in the Oscars when they show your photograph in the 'Dearly Departed' montage. It's nice but doesn't make much difference to your earning potential.

KING DAVID ONE

David was one of the sons of the Saintly and Good Margaret and, like a trainspotter who gains their love of noting down serial numbers from a parent, David found he loved God too. He wasn't one of those who say they're religious but just go to a church on Sunday and mime along to the hymns while thinking about what to have for tea. Oh no – our Davie was big on the whole shebang. He invited the Augustinians, Cistercians and Premonstratensians.* If your God-bothering group ended in 'ian', you were in!

David wanted these new monks on the block to improve the morals and character of the place. One way of doing this was to worship pieces of the cross that Jesus had died on. These 'holy roods' were collected and those in charge looked at the gigantic pile of wood that was enough to build an arc and quietly got rid of some of them before anyone 'twigged'. These relics gave their name to an area in Edinburgh that would be mispronounced down the centuries. It's Holyrood.

LEWIS CHESSMEN

Some of the more unusual and striking artefacts of around this time are the Lewis Chessmen – small chess pieces that are in the shape of small men. Some of the figures are face-palming, others have wild, staring eyes.

* Real names.

One bites down on his shield. That's what playing chess does to you. Some have jokingly suggested that as they were produced in the Outer Hebrides they should perhaps have made pieces for the game of draughts.* Luckily few make this joke nowadays as, after 800 years, it is beginning to pall.

WILLIAM THE LION

In Eleven Seventy Oatcake, King William followed his calling and invaded Canada. (No, it was England, silly!) A great victory was celebrated at Alnwick. Only joking! It was an embarrassing defeat and Willy was captured. Peace then broke out.

This wasn't William's only contribution to Scottish history. He had seen the nice white and blue flag the country had, but he wanted more. He wanted his own special flag, so marketing agencies were invited to tender and they came up with a design that said it all: a lion standing up saying, 'Put 'em up, put 'em up!' in a very non-cowardly way. It was called the lion rampant and this royal standard was a proud symbol that echoed down the centuries on items such as car stickers, mouse mats and underpants.

The rampant lion proudly joined the pantheon of Scottish national symbols. It stood alongside the national plant: the thistle (only Scotland could have a national plant that is joogy (joogy), unwelcoming and is basically an unwanted weed). Another national Scottish symbol is, of

* Because it's windy there.

course, the unicorn,* a mythical creature in the form of a horse with a narwhal-like horn poking out its forehead.

AULD (AULD) ALLIANCE

Towards the end of the Thirteenth Century Oatcake, Scotland signed an agreement making France its official best friend forever. They had sleepovers, held hands going to the swimming pool and opened up trade exchanges. They also promised to help each other out if war should break out with You Know Who,** but there was hardly any chance of that happening, right?

Scotland imported huge amounts of wine from its new bezzie mate: *vin blanc*, *vin rouge* and *vin diesel*, which led to an increase in bench pressing and the wearing of tight t-shirts. In return, France got the *Sunday Post*. C'est tout?

Actually, they got more than that. They got people. Scotspersons went over to France, with some becoming mercenaries. Getting paid to fight? They couldn't believe their luck, and although there was a risk of death, what was that to a fat pay packet and regular fighting?

* It really is! Look it up.

** England.

9 THE WARS OF INDEPENDENCE

OR

WHAUR'S YOUR WULLIE WALLACE NOO?

There is a strong tradition in Scottish history of grasping defeat, crisis, trauma and disaster in the face of victory. Especially in football – Gary McAllister, why didn't you wait until the ball was still?!* But one of the biggest disasters was caused by a man they called King Alexander Three, in Twelve Eighty Oatcake.

KING ALEXANDER THREE: THE WRONG DECISION

King Alexander Three was well regarded as kings go. (And unfortunately for him, he did go.) He'd beaten the Vikings at Largs and acquired the Western Isles in an early form of Monopoly. This was good going. He hadn't died young, which was a result too. Not only that, he'd made a family, though when his wife Margaret died and all his children died this disappeared but, needing some heirs, Alex remarried and 'got back in the saddle', as it were.

Now one stormy night the wind did blow and the rain did fall and good King Alex was separated by the large and wet expanse of the Firth of Forth from his wife. A wife he keenly wished to 'visit', as it were. The bridge hadn't been invented by a Scotsperson yet, so he would have to take the ferry. The ferryperson wasn't convinced of the wisdom of this plan and cited many health and safety issues with crossing a large area of choppy water on a stormy night. The king nodded and said he had made

* It's a football thing. Don't look up '1990 Penalty miss England v Scotland'. It'll bring up a lot of pain.

a good point, and then told the ferryperson that if he didn't row him over he'd chop off the ferryman's head. Convinced of the strength of his randy king's arguments, the ferryperson set off into the turmoil of this dark and tempestuous night. He turned back when he realised he'd left the by now humourless king on the shore.

Off they went. The boat was tossed hither and thither, but they made it and Alexander set off on his horse along the coastal path.

And that's where he came a cropper.

On the rocks this ragged rascal ran out of luck. To add a supernatural element to this sad tale, his death was predicted by the seer Thomas the Rhymer. Thomas had written:

> There will be a king called Alex,
> Who one night will ride off for some sex.
> His horse will lose its footing,
> A calamity will occur there can be no doubting.
> And who knows what will happen to Scotland next.

He wasn't a great rhymer, all the timer, was our Thomas.

But it wasn't all bad news, as King Alex's death was to lead to that great pastime of the Scots: fighting. And not only that – fighting England.

ENGLISH KING EDWARD ONE

England's King Edward One was known by several names, only some of which can be printed in a family 'history' book. One was 'Longshanks', due to the length of his legs

– 'long' meaning 'not short' and 'shanks' being an old word for 'legs'. His children called him Daddy Longlegs, not because of his leg length but because he flittered around the bedroom at night keeping everyone awake.

After Alexander's demise there was no clear successor to the throne in Scotland who was alive, so Edward was given the job as adjudicator. He had work to do as plenty of people wanted to be king. Being king got you a better standard of living. For example, the bedbugs would bow before sinking their teeth into your tender fleshy parts.

There were thirteen candidates who thought they had the Saltire Factor. One of them could play the trumpet while balancing on a unicycle, another could sing the *Marseillaise* backwards – in French! But Edward Big Leggy plumped for John Balliol, whose talent was saying he didn't mind having England as an overlord. Soon he was through to the final round where he was made King John One of Scotland.

However, things didn't work out and soon war was had between Scotland and England. Those who liked battling bit down on their fists to stop themselves yelling out 'Yasss!' During this time, Edward became unpopular, especially in Berwick-upon-Tweed, when he set the good townsfolk on fire. They had not invited him to their gala day (there was a mix-up in the organising committee over who was sending out the invites) and Eddy took umbrage – Sir Geoffrey d'Umbrage – who brought the matches.

DUNBAR AND DUSTED

At the Battle of Dunbar, in Twelve Ninety Oatcake, the Scots army had – as the military analysts would best put it – 'their arses handed to them'. To call Dunbar a rout is to do the word a disservice. It was a rrrrrrout. King John was stripped of his royal insignia in front of everyone by his English counterpart. If Edward Lengthy Trousers had pulled John's pants up his backside in a classic wedgie, it could not have been more humiliating. As a result, Balliol was called 'Toom Tabard' (Toom Tabard) and those who broke into his castle while he was away were called 'Toom Raiders'. John was told to get to France where he loved the exotic cheeses and wines and long lunches. He would bore French people by telling them, 'I used to be a king you know', before falling off his bar stool.

During his campaigns north of the border Edward had used a large siege engine called the War Wolf. Unfortunately, due to a communication failure the first version that was ordered was a Werewolf. This didn't impress Edward one bit, as a Scotsperson hadn't invented silver bullets yet and so the wolf was chomping its way through his knights. Eventually Edwardo employed the services of a trio of pigs who lured the hairy beast into a boiling pot of water.

Scots nobles reacted speedily to this outrageous Englishman coming up and killing people and immediately rushed to pledge allegiance to him. They added their names to the 'Ragman's Roll', which was a name for the list. Some of the Scots nobles didn't treat the process with enough respect. You know who you are Mickeaux Mouse, Dunald Ducke and Hugh J'Arse.

WILLIAM AND ANDY

With Scotland under the oppressive rule of an invading force there could only be one man who could lead Scotland to victory. But he would have to wait his turn while there was some more fighting between Scotland and England. This fighting was done under the command of probably the most famous alliterative freedom fighter of all time: William Wallace, and his partner in arms, Andy 'Andrew' Murray. Murray had a great forehand axe smash and Wallace had a sword that was longer than some boats. He was to Scotland what Eddie the Eagle was to England, centuries later: brave, popular and famous for doing something daft. Taking on the might of the large medieval army of England was not deemed wise in many people's books, especially those marked 'surviving'. But in the plucky way a pub team of accountants and taxi drivers takes on a Scottish Premiership side in the cup, Wallace was also ready for the challenge.

BRAVEHEART BATTLES #1: STIRLING BRIDGE

At the end of this battle, the Scots slumped away in despondency. Then people told them they'd actually won and they quickly roused themselves into the party spirit. That's the thing with medieval battles, it wasn't always clear if you'd won or not, but being alive was always a result and at the end of the day the boys done good. Drink was had, feasts were eaten and the skin of one of the English knights was made into a belt. This limited-edition item was available in the battle site's gift shop at a very reasonable 10 groats.

Murray and Wallace had won a famous battle, but in classic Scottish style soon grabbed defeat from the jaws of victory. When his soldiers heard Murray was dying, they thought he was dying for a pint. He probably was, but the inconvenience of having a mortal wound prevented any swallying. Wallace accepted his partner's death, saying, 'I suppose they'll make a film about just me, then.' He was to be correct in that. A film that was – spoiler alert! – not to have a happy ending, but it wasn't all over yet.

BRAVEHEART BATTLES #2: FALKIRK

Edward One was not a good loser and sent his troops northwards. He was not going to let this cheeky monkey Wallace make a fool outta him, no sirree! He led his troops up, down and around the country while Wallace peeked out from behind trees and did that impudent thing with the waggling hands beside the ears while wiggling his tongue before running off. Finally, the Edster caught up with him and it was decided to have a battle at Falkirk.

Edward pulled a sneaky one, adding strings to his arsenal by using Welsh bowmen to fire their arrows at the Scots. Despite Scottish cries of 'That's not fair!' and 'Why didn't we think of that?', the Welsh kept on shooting their pointy bits of wood at their soft flesh. The best thing to do when faced with bowmen is to:

1. Run away
2. Quickly invent armoured personnel carriers.

Unfortunately, the Scots did something else – they died. The Scottish nobles had brought their cavalry, but didn't like being commanded by a ned like Wallace and departed quickly when it looked like a defeat was looming. Wallace was hurt by this, but not as hurt as he would be later.

BETRAYED

While staying near Glasgow, Wallace was betrayed and captured while still in his jim-jams. He was taken to London and, although excited to see the Tower of London, was unable to purchase a fridge magnet as they chopped him up into bits. King Eddie had regarded Wallace as a traitor and had wanted him dead. Wallace's defence plea of being a first offender was refused. He was led to the gallows and, still hurting at his treatment,* was hanged, drawn and quartered.

Eduardo had got his man. Scotland's 'Braveheart, Lungs & Spleen' was gone. It was bad for Scotland, but even more so for Wallace. Even his famed powers of resistance were unable to overcome the adversity of being dead, although as his head was rolling away it was heard to shout, 'I'll get you for this, you big-legged numpty!'

* The court artist had made his nose far too big.

King Ed had famously described Scotland as 'ane fert of my erse', which was harsh as he also ruled Belgium.* It was on his way to Scotland for yet another bit of fighting that he died in Thirteen Oatcake. He was known as the 'Hammer of the Scots', which was apt, as when he died most of Scotland celebrated by getting absolutely hammered. He was to be followed in the time-honoured way by a successor, his son, Edward Two.

STONE OF DESTINY (OR SCONE)

One of Scotland's most valuable artefacts is a lump of stone that was used as a pillow by Jacob in biblical times and then transported to Ireland before ending up in Perthshire. That's Scotland right there: placing great value on the nonsensical. This is the country whose chief tourist product is a non-existent dinosaur. Whoops, what was said earlier? Oh, nothing to see here, let's move on. And don't worry, there's *definitely* a Santa.

This stone is called the Stone of Destiny or the Stone of Scone, which does not refer to those raisin-filled baked treats that go well with jam and cream, but after the place outside Perth called Scone, that the Romans had great difficulty in pronouncing properly. It's *Scone*, okay?

The history of The Stone is simple: anyone becoming King or Queen of Scotland would sit on the stone when they were getting crowned. This led to their mothers informing them of the risk of contracting haemorrhoids from sitting

* Sorry Belgium, too often the butt of fart jokes.

on a cold surface. Wiser kings got themselves a cushion to avoid this problem. (Or made sure their mothers were sitting quite far back and out of hearing range.)

In Thirteen Oatcake, the stone was robbed from its rightful place under the bums of Scottish monarchs by thiefy King Edward One, and taken against its will to that den of inequity and men and women dressed in bejewelled suits. Yes, London. It would pain anyone whose heart was not a stone to think of that forlorn and heartbroken rock being hauled away down the long and lonely road, with each turn of the wagon wheel taking it further away from its tranquil home and other stones it had come to call friends, its metal cage soaked with stone tears.

Centuries later, the Stone of Scone was returned to its rightful place: Edinburgh. Eh? Well it was close to Scone, if you don't get caught up in traffic. It was taken to Edinburgh Castle and placed near to the gift shop. To cast your eyes on this much-written-about treasure you have to queue for ages behind hundreds of tourists who photograph themselves, the information panels, and themselves looking at the information panels. The novelty never wears off.

In its presence reactions are awed. 'Aw, is that it?' and, 'Aw man, we queued for that?', they exclaim sadly, having wasted valuable time that could have been better spent photographing themselves elsewhere. Thankfully, no photography is allowed in The Stone's room or it might be used on a more stone-to-skull basis.

BRUCE ALMIGHTY

With Wallace in pieces, the way was clear for someone else to continue the fighting between Scotland and England. This man was Robert the Bruce – technically incorrect as he was only *a* Bruce, not *the* Bruce. The others in the family didn't mind him hogging the surname though, as his exploits would echo down the centuries.

Robert had initially faffed around and didn't know what to do. It's like when you leave university and you're not sure if you want to get a job and earn some money or if you'd rather join some friends who are travelling. This can go on until your parents get sick of you and you get an ultimatum. Robert's parents told him: tidy up your room, or become monarch. So he decided to be king and stabbed one of his rivals in a church and asked a pal, who happened to be an archbishop, to make him king, which he did. This career option is not open to all, it should be said.

Robert found himself chased and harried and had to hide. The English called him King Hobbe (no idea why) and with his dwindling support he was forced to take refuge in dung heaps and caves (where his own voice would echo down the cave). Luckily for him, Scotland was really big at the time and there were plenty of places to hole up as he was chased hither and thither.

But a fictitious encounter with a made-up spider encouraged him to continue. By not watching a spider try again and again to make a web, he resolved to continue his struggle. To be honest, he was probably driven daft by the stress of being pursued at this point, so a non-existent spider telling him to keep going was the least of his worries.

Bruce was good at the fighting, but didn't really want a big battle, however, when English King Edward Two marched up to Scotland to relieve himself on Stirling Castle* in Thirteen Oatcake, as he had nothing else on that week, Bruce thought, 'What the hell?'

THE GREATEST DAY EVER

What was probably Scotland's greatest ever victory took place near the visitor centre at Bannockburn in Thirteen Oatcake. The battle took place at midsummer, before the schools broke up for the summer holidays, and was split over two days on police advice, to avoid traffic congestion issues.

When the teams lined up it was found the Scots were outnumbered three to one. 'The Bruce' asked the English if they thought these odds were fair and offered to wait until they got more soldiers to give themselves a chance. What a guy! King Robert marshalled his forces so well that a home win was almost guaranteed. It was like Murray vs Henman, except you got to hit your opponent over the head with something large and metallic rather than tennis balls.

The evening before the main battle, the great King Robert was attacked by a lone English knight called Sir Edward de Bonehead. De Bonehead spotted the bright yellow

* Definitely check this in the edit.

tabard* of the Scottish King. The bold English knight saw an opportunity to finish off the brave King Robert and charged at him. But the most excellent King Robert rose in his stirrups and planted an axe in his opponent's head, giving him a headache worse than a night on the mead shots. The wondrous King Robert turned to his supporters and, showing them his splintered axe, remarked, 'That was a good axe that', which led to much backslapping and hearty laughing by his entourage keen not to feel the axe's sharp bit on their own heads if they didn't laugh hard enough. The ace King Robert's cool witticism in the heat of the moment was later adopted by that other Great Scot: Sir Sean of Connery in the James Bond films, although Sir Sean was not actually at Bannockburn, having to do his milk round that day.

At the start of the main battle the next day, the Scots advanced towards the English lines. The English felt alarm rise in their throats and something else move south inside their bodkins. Suddenly the Scots army stopped and dropped to its knees. Had someone lost a contact lens? 'Should have gone to Eyeglass Savers,' one of them quipped to a nervous chuckle from several of the soldiers

* No, he wasn't earning extra cash by working as a cleaner. Around this time, knights wore long cloth garments over their armour as it helped identify them – it made collecting the important corpses quicker – and also for sponsorship purposes. You could get a lot of company logos on a tabard. Those funerals wouldn't pay for themselves!

within earshot. Others looked around for tumbleweed, but there was none to be had.

There was no laughing when the battle kicked off, it being a typical medieval affair: lots of pennants, lances, thundering hooves, limbs being severed, cleaving in twain, shouting of 'gadzooks!',* and merry jesters jesting.** As the battle hung in the balance, the English spotted what they thought was another army approaching over a hill. That was it. They abandoned ship. Panicking, they fled. The new army was of little harm to them, a coach party from Aberdeen who had found the visitor centre shut and had wandered over looking for the toilets.

English King Edward Two of England saw his forces utterly trounced, his army thoroughly rrrrrouted, and his men overwhelmingly beaten, most literally. The carnage was terrible and many brave men – plus some very cowardly ones – were killed. A field covered in thousands of butchered dead took the edge off a lovely summer's day, but the crowd went home happy: a home win.

With his army in tatters, King Edward Two got his horse to leg it and it was said they never stopped until they reached Dunbar. By the time he got away, Eduardo was bursting for the toilet, having not gone before leaving.

* No idea.

** There weren't as many jesters as there should have been. There was a diary mix-up and many were at a silver wedding anniversary in Peebles.

Although some said he had met his Bannockburn that day, he was just glad to meet his water loo …*

Edward would eventually die in terrible agony in Thirteen Oatcake after allegedly having a red-hot poker inserted into his rear end. 'I think he got the point,' King Robert said, wittily and to thunderous laughter.

AFTERWARDS

After the glories of Bannockburn, war between Scotland and England continued for a while. Like a football manager who wins a cup but the following season sees his team hover near to the relegation zone, King Robert wasn't finding much of a honeymoon period. Ruling wasn't that easy. He sent his brother to invade Ireland in the kind of colonial expansion that many at the time, and since, have deemed 'daft'. The Irish weren't overly chuffed to have foreigners turning up and they were less chuffed when the Scots ate all the food during a bad harvest. You know what it's like when you go to a tapas restaurant and the dishes you've ordered end up at the far end of the table, and you can't get to them as everyone finds the food you've picked delicious and you sit there grim-faced chomping on the Brussels sprouts? That's kind of what Ireland being invaded by Scotland was like.

* Found that tumbleweed!

WELL, I DECLARE

In Thirteen Oatcake one of Scotland's most important documents was produced. The recipe for Irn-Bru was carefully stowed away in a secret place known only to a few members of the Iron Barr family. Once this was done, the king and nobles and earls and dukes and barons and – more importantly – someone with a pen, sat down and wrote the Declaration of Arbroath. It was a letter to the Pope, and it said:

Dear Pope,
Please can we be moved further from Montrose?
Best wishes,
The People of Arbroath

The king, although seeing the merits, demanded something a bit more … relevant to the wider political and religious situation. The second draft went:

Dear Pope,
Please can we have peace and be a country on our own, and can Brave King Robert not be sent to eternal damnation on account of the small matter of him killing someone in a church (someone who deserved it by the way) and being excommunicated.
Best wishes,
The People of Scotland
P.S. Can we be moved further from Carnoustie?

The Declaration echoed down the centuries and its stirring evocation of human rights was used as the centrepiece for many tea towels and authentic archive-looking parchments available in the many gift shops that run down Edinburgh's Royal Mile.

PEACE

Eventually, in Thirteen Oatcake, the cries of 'Gie's peace!' (Gie's peace) were finally heard and the nation's hobby of fighting England was halted by a peace treaty. However, no one's hearts were really in it and when Edward Two died in Thirteen Oatcake it was back to the good old days of war when Scotland invaded England.

King Robert the Greatest was not able to enjoy all the fighting as he sadly joined the ranks of the immortal by dying in Thirteen Oatcake. He'd lived a successful life: becoming king, killing a man in a church (who obviously deserved it), killing many English in battle, rescuing his sister from a cage suspended from outside a castle's walls and establishing a country's independence.

Honestly, how many of us can say that?

A TALE OF TWO EDS AND A DAVE

Robert the Bruce's son was called David and he assumed the throne was his. Although kids grew up fast in those days, being 4 years old was deemed a bit too young to

rule Scotland effectively. Wales maybe, but not Scotland.*
So some guardians were appointed to look after the country while he grew up and stopped behaving like a child.

In England, the king was now Edward Three. He was unhappy with Scotland. No reason, just didn't like the place. You know the way you meet someone and you quickly just know you're not going to like them? Well Ed didn't even meet Scotland. He just took a fancy to disliking it. He supported the actions of Edward the Balliol, who was the son of the former king, King John the Balliol. Edward the Balliol was the man who wanted to be king and his arrival in Scotland in Thirteen Oatcake astonishingly saw some fighting between Scotland and England. He cheekily took the crown for himself and, as King Edward (Scotland), he swore loyalty to King Edward (England). Luckily, this saw the end of any more fighting between Scotland and England.**

Soon it was time for David to become the king. He wasn't too popular and was told to get to France and to France he did go. He stayed for a while, absorbing the culture and language, before returning in Thirteen Oatcake, where he duly invaded England in order to start some fighting between the two countries. What was with kings of this time? Couldn't they just put their feet up and do some hunting or fishing and flirt with the ladies-in-waiting? Oh no, they had to keep on fighting and dying.

* Obviously a joke. No one could rule Wales. Then or now. Yeah.

** Of course it didn't.

David was beaten at a battle called Neville's Cross, so named because wouldn't you be if your land was covered in post-battle blood and guts and stuff?

David was taken to London where he discovered life wasn't so bad, he was able to get all the souvenirs he wanted. He was in no rush to get back to Scotland. That said a lot about being monarch of the country: it was preferable to be held captive in England rather than be king in Scotland.

10 THE STEWARTS

OR

SEE YOU, KING JIMMY

The rule of the Stewart dynasty began in Thirteen Oatcake with the kingship of King Robert Two. He was an old, old man when he finally got his bum on the throne. He was 54. If nowadays your fifties are the new thirties, back then your fifties were the new deadies. But our Robert lived until he was an astounding 74, which was tantamount to being a wizard to the simpletons of the era. Rob Two made many pronouncements along the lines of 'Pah, in my day The Plague was a proper plague, not like this modern rubbish infection. Pass the *Sunday Post*, will you?' This endeared him to the wrinkly old peasants who thought this sort of inane gibberish indicated wisdom.

King Robert thought it only fair that he got to wage war with England, and so he did, and at a place called Otterburn the Scots surprised their opponents – and themselves – by winning. That was, like, twice in a century – crazeee!

When he eventually died, everyone was sad apart from his son Robert Three, who became King Robert Three. Robert had been born John, but changed his name to Robert as John had bad connotations. He'd heard people in America called their toilets 'johns'. This name change did not go down well with Robert's younger brother, Robert, who quite fancied the crown himself. There was a lot of family infighting which we won't go into as it's too complicated for anyone to research.

As a king, Robert Three had to deal with the Wolf of Badenoch, who was kidding no one. Yes, he would howl at the moon, eat woodland people's grannies and pee on lamp posts but he was really a man. Old King Bob was not a happy chappy. He was prone to melancholia and low spirits, a condition known in Scotland as 'life'. To be fair, he did have a bad time: he had been kicked by a horse in the Trossachs, had one son starved to death in a castle and another who was captured by pirates and kept in a castle – by the English no less! – for eighteen years. It would have made for a good epic series on Netflix, but sadly for Robert it was real life. Eventually he gave up the ghost, and became one. He wrote (before he died):

Please bury me, I beg you, in a midden.

He was buried in Paisley. Make your own jokes.

THE HIGHLANDS

It shouldn't be thought that the Scots liked only to fight the English. They were more than happy to knock seven shades of sharn (sharn) out of each other too. Highlanders fought Lowlanders, and in the Highlands one clan would fight the other and the clans would have infighting, and so on. It was all good fun and not too many died.

THE TARTAN ARMY

In Fourteen Twenty Oatcake, 12,000 Scottish foot soldiers were in France. No, it wasn't a World Cup but a chance to mix some variety into the fighting with England because these Scots were in France to go into battle with the English. That's dedication to the cause – and inventive too. The Hundred Years War was on and the Scots were worried that it'd be over without them getting involved. The eventual victory over the English king, King Henry Five, was a famous one that echoed down the centuries.

CASTLES

If an Englishman's home is his castle, in the Middle Ages a Scots nobleman's home *was* a castle. If you were kind of a big deal you just had to live in a fortified dwelling place with the obligatory moat, ramparts, dungeons and a handy place from which to tip your sharn (sharn) onto the nearby villagers.

Castles were great for keeping people out. If you didn't want your moat cleaned you just pulled up the drawbridge, tipped boiling oil on their heads and laughed as the hawkers went away disgruntled – and burnt. The trouble arose when you wanted *out*. That opened up the weak spot and a smart attacker would wait until, say, the castle's owner fancied a fish supper, and as soon as the gates were open – wham! – a bang on the head of the drawbridge operations executive and in they went. Once inside, they took control and threw out the current occupants. Bingo, they could then enjoy their new seat of power and laugh at those castleless losers.

Until one night, when they decided to have something different for tea, and fancied a fish supper …

MORE DEATH

In Fourteen Oatcake, two things hit Scotland hard: weather and disease. It got colder (no one noticed at first as it struck during the summer holidays) and wetter. These are two words you never want to hear near each other in Scotland. Then came something even worse: The Black Death, which was also known as The Plague, and which was back again. There was very little to do but pray and keel over, both of which were done with true Scottish grit, and a fair bit of moaning about the local council's lack of action.

It got so bad that children were unable to attend school. Those carrying the sick notes to school died, so those dying didn't get their message to the school and the truant officer came round to see what was happening and then they got sick and died, so the HR office sent staff out to find out where all the truant officers were and then when they got ill the management team had to investigate, and when they started dropping like the fleas that had brought the bloody disease in the first place then the senior management executive team thought 'sod that for a lark' and legged it to the golf course. Where they caught The Plague from their caddies.

War is a terrible thing, but at least you've got the chance of winning the hand (and a whole lot more if she's amenable) of a fair young maiden if you conquer a fellow knight in battle. If you get The Plague then the woman of your dreams seems to have other things on that night and doesn't rush to answer your wassailing under her window.

It was a truly terrible time. And this was in a period *before* football had been invented by a Scotsperson.

TRADING PLACES

Scotland, around this time, was able to do good business with the continent of Europe. It was thought best to sell things to Europe as it wasn't too far away and they had warehouses full of booze just waiting to be loaded into a galley for the return journey. America* hadn't been invented yet, and so 'trade' over the 'pond' was not 'possible'.

This 'trade' was carried out by towns that were called 'burghs' and so those trading in pig meat were 'hamburghers', those in vegetables were 'veggieburghers' and those afraid to deal with foreigners were 'chickenburghers'. Their achievements in establishing a peaceful network of commerce echoed down the centuries.

UNLUCKY JIMS

One morning around this time, one of the great and the good of the Scottish nobility woke up with a start.** This noble realised Scotland hadn't had a king called James, so one was rustled up. He was followed by five similarly named male monarchs, each of whom expired in the following manner:

* Despire being mentioned a few pages ago.
** How the start had gotten into his bed is another story. Ho-ho.

James One – stabbed in a sewer
James Two – blown up by a cannon (his own)
James Three – killed in battle (by his own nobles)
James Four – killed in battle (with England)
James Five – died of anguish
James Six – old age.

So, even for monarchs, dying horribly around this time wasn't uncommon.

In Fourteen Oatcake an event took place that showed that underneath the intrigue of the royal court lay a seam of nasty horribleness. At a dinner held in Edinburgh's Edinburgh Castle, the teenage Earl of Douglas was invited. During the evening of banter, bonhomie and bon viveurness, a black bull's head was presented to the earl and his younger brother. As table centrepieces go it wasn't that aesthetically pleasing, but decorative tastes were different then. But, ah, this wasn't merely decorative, it was A Sign. A Sign that someone at the table was not going to be around for coffee and mints. The Earl of Douglas soon became the Earl of Headless, as he was taken away and literally given the chop. The event became known as the Black Dinner, and was to echo down the centuries.

NAMES

Around this time, it was common for notable figures to have nicknames. For example, the Earl of Douglas was known as 'James the Gross', the Earl of Crawford was called 'Earl Beardie' and the Earl of East Lothian was called Billy, as the person who came up with the nicknames for everyone had died of guess what.

A RENAISSANCE KING

In the Fifteenth Century Oatcake, Europe was in thrall to the delights of the Renaissance. Paintings were painted, sculptures were sculpted and intricate curtains were drawn. Colour and beauty were abundant, serfs and peasants could often be seen without pig sharn on their faces. Glory days of culture abounded.

In Nineteen Eighty Oatcake, this book's writer was asked in a history test, 'Was King James Four a Renaissance king?' He didn't know the right answer then but with the internet now available he can say: Yes, James Four *was* a Renaissance king. It's too late to avoid a resit but it's not too late to be included in this tome.

James Four went for the Renaissance big time. While other kings of the time went for the hunting and eating chicken drumsticks part of being a monarch, James went all cultural. He commissioned architectural works, he watched plays,* and he set up the first printing press in Scotland. Yes, nobody could read, but they had books. That's got to count for something.

* One of the plays was entitled ane Pleasant Satyre of the Thrie Estaitis, which sold like 'ane plate o' hotcakes' and received 'Ane five-star revue in Ye Scoatsman newspapyre'.

At Stirling, Jimbo built the Great Hall, the Alright Foyer and Downright Bloody Awful Car Park. Hey, even Renaissance kings have off-days. He had an impressive warship built, which took a while as all 428 editions of the magazine had to be collected first. This mighty vessel was given the name *St Michael*, in case it had to be returned within twenty-eight days (with proof of purchase).

Education was also in fashion and around this time Scotland had three esteemed seats of learning at Aberdeen, Glasgow and St Andrews. While good, it was felt more young Scots should get a chance of taking a load off while getting some learning, so they brought in more chairs and never looked back. These universities were not the dynamic, innovative centres of excellence that exist nowadays, where sheep are cloned and Bosuns are found in space. These were dour and dull institutions where the students had to suffer hour after hour of dry verbosity from tutors eking out their allotted time until they could get back to their quarters to continue 'research' into their 'etchings' with their young students.

But although being arty-farty, James Four didn't lose sight of his traditional Scottish kingly duties: to fight with England. And lose.

FLODDEN

For those still with us, it can be easily seen that Scottish history is filled with utter disasters, but none compare to the sheer sharn-fest that was Flodden. As had happened in the past, the king of the day thought it an idea to risk the lives and limbs of his subjects in a battle over something or other. In this case, it was over Scotland supporting France in a war against King Henry Eight's England.

The large Scots army* marched south and the Battle of Flodden actually took place at a place called Branxton. This pleased the Branxtonburghers, who were worried about the negative effects on house prices.

The Scots took up the worst position possible: in front of the English army. If they'd only hidden in the many woods available – but no. At one point, the English troops were moving and the Scots artillery wanted to fire, but the king thought this unchivalrous and stopped them. That's what made those days of chivalry and honour. You might be killed, but at least it was done *properly*.

It's not known how many died at the battle but it was A Lot, possibly as much as 10,000. King James Four also pegged it that day. However, it wasn't all bad; we got a lovely song to mark the occasion called 'The Flowers of the Forest'. It was said no bird ever flew over the battlefield; it is true, they were all killed too.

* That's a numerous army of Scots, not an army composed of hefty chaps, although some were quite fond of the pie.

BORDERING ON MADNESS

Flodden is near to the Borders, one of the current regions of modern-day Scotland. It is so named as it 'borders' England. The Borders are populated with towns with their own distinct character and flavour. Some are named after famous residents: Jed Burgh, Mel Rose and Newt Onstboswells.

Many Borders towns have a fierce rivalry, focused on the game of rugby. A tournament is played in Mel Rose's town called the Mel Rose Sevens, in which teams consist of seven players rather than the normal fifteen. It has been scurriously suggested that this came about in the first tournament when half the team were too hung-over to play. This is a scandalous slur on the good folk of the Borders. If half the team were hung-over, the whole team would be hung-over – that's what a team is.

Another tradition of the Borders is the Riding of the March Hares. In order to reassert the town's boundaries, local people gallop about on large rabbit-type ruminants, carrying flags. Eventually this ritual will be replaced by the Satnaving of the Marches, where delivery lorries drive around before coming to rest on a too-narrow bridge.

KING JAMES FIVE

As king, King James Five did something quite extraordinary: he talked to the great unwashed. Big deal, you might say, everyone was unwashed in them days. True. But he talked to the *really* unwashed: the populace. He dressed up in poor clothes and wandered about chatting away, asking the peasants things like:

> 'And what is it you do?'
> 'Yes, I think it will brighten up later, don't you?'
> 'Why haven't you invented paint yet? This place stinks of sharn.'

Being a Scottish king of the time, of course he couldn't avoid war with England and when he forged a bond with France – by forging his own bond, if you get my drift, by marrying a French lady, Mary of Guise – King Henry Eight lost his head* and war was had. James Five took to his bed, not long for the world. The fighting between Scotland and England resulted in a heavy loss – no way! – at Solway Moss.

The disaster made an already ill King James get another sick note. On his deathbed – a range no longer available from any supplier these days – he heard the news that he had a newborn daughter. He famously said, 'A girl? We'll still call her James though?' and then expired. His daughter was not called James. She was given the name Mary and her name would echo down the centuries as she was going to be a Queen of Scots.

* Not quite like his wives.

ROUGH WOOING

Rough and wooing. Not words that normally go together, but England's Henry Eight wasn't normal. (Even in those days of yore, killing off your wives to get your own way wasn't quite seen as completely acceptable. Was it political correctness gone mad? No.)

This Rough Wooing came about as one of fat king Henry's wives produced a son called Edward, and Henry wanted Edward to marry the young Scottish princess called Mary. When the Scots showed some uncertainty about it – in the way proud parents sniff at their daughter's suitor coming into the house wearing an Anarchist t-shirt and smelling of potatoes – Henry immediately launched a military campaign. By attacking the country about to deny his son his day at the altar, he hoped to convince them to think again. A bit like a suitor saying, 'Go out with me or I'll burn your house down.' Charming it was not.

This naturally led to some fighting between Scotland and England. Edinburgh was attacked and the smell of burning tea towels could be detected in Shetland. There was some more battling for a bit, mixed in with some peace, then in Fifteen Forty Oatcake some young Protestants* in St Andrews were in dispute with a religious figure called Cardinal Beaton. They wore disguises, but this was the days before shops had fancy dress outfits to wear and so they came as stonemasons, who dress Exactly Like Everyone Else. But, despite this, they got past the visitor

* Humans who protest, not ants.

centre staff and into St Andrews' Castle, where Beaton was living and they killed him, hanging him outside in a bed sheet. This was the era before non-bio washing powders and it took days to get that sheet whiter than white again.

As a pal does in a fight, Scotland's bezzie mates – the French – jumped in to help and besieged the town. When Big Fat Henry Eight died in Fifteen Forty Oatcake there was a feeling that this warring would cease. Fat chance. It continued, and in Fifteen Forty Oatcake you would not believe what happened. The Scots lost a battle! A proper doing,* at a quaintly named place you'd imagine pixies gambolling in the pre-dawn mist: Pinkie Cleugh. The English now occupied much of the south of Scotland, including Haddington. They would have taken Tranent but they weren't that desperate for a fight.

This Rough Wooing was proving to be too rough, and the young Mary was told to allez to France, which she did.** Around this time, things were to be reformed and this project was given a suitable name: the Reformation, which pleased its supporters but saddened its opponents, who didn't want things changed. But one set of people were going to be disappointed. And reformed.***

* From A Wooing To A Doing – a catchy title for any historians out there struggling to pep up their worthy tomes on this period. Usual finder's fees apply.

** She'll be back though, don't worry.

*** Belated spoiler alert.

11 THE REFORMATION

OR

YOU'LL HAVE HAD YOUR HOLY SEE

After centuries believing in Jesus one way, the Protesting Ants – no, humans, they were humans! Course they were.* They decided to believe in Jesus, but in a different way. They were like a boy who stops a game of football and marches off with the ball when things aren't going his way, and then orders the players to start playing rugby and sets fire to those still wanting to play football.** When presented with the option of joining the new Protestant Church or being pelted with flaming stones and having their house set aflame, most thought, 'What the hell, how bad can it be?'

The Protestant reformists ran under the campaign banner of 'You're Not Here to Enjoy Yourself' and, by God, no one did. They attacked the pleasures in life with a zeal that made it look as if those taking part *were* enjoying themselves, which is the sort of irony smart-arsed writers like to present to show how clever they are.

Austerity was now in. Christmas was banned. Can you imagine? No carol singers, no mistletoe, no secret Santas, no office night outs sitting next to Kevin with the body odour from IT … actually, that sounds okay.

And it wasn't just Christmas. There was no Easter – no eggs! – plus there was to be no singing in church, no drinking, no gambling, no fun. Even the *Sunday Post* was chastised for its inclusion of the merry adventures of that irascible rascal Poor Wullie. With his bubonic rat Rheumy

* You'd never be able to hear an ant protesting about anything. Ridiculous idea.

** Some of those non-believers were as tortured as that analogy.

and best pal Skeletal Bob, he would run into all sorts of fun and trouble with Church Constable PC Prod. Wullie was eventually burnt at the stake for knocking over a bust of John Knox with his catapult.

PEACE, LOVE AND UNDERSTANDING

Now, you would think with all this Christian stuff being talked about there would be plenty forgiveness and tolerance being advocated. Nuh-uh, not on your nelly. The two sides – Protestant and Catholic – were at loggerheads (loggerheads). Around this time, someone thought that if they transferred all their mutual bad feeling into a sporting outlet it would help divulge the nasty feelings and allow this to be the only focus of any lingering resentment. Some brainstorming was carried out and it was decided to form two football teams whose exploits would echo down the centuries. But more of them later.

GOLF AND CANNIBALISM

Around this time, two horrendous calamities that would turn anyone's stomach came to light. One involved the hitting of balls, the other, the eating of them.

Around Fifteen Oatcake, a Scotsperson invented golf. The evidence for this does not need enquiring, suffice it to say that if you can think of any other country that would devise a pointless exercise involving something small being hit over and over across windswept countryside then please do send it in to the usual address.

Golf nowadays is mainly played by men aged over 50, or those who dress like they want to be. Of course, women do play it but are received in male-only club houses like a radioactive leper who has bad breath.* Golf thrives in Scotland with more clubs than you can swing a club at. It's said you can play your way right across East Lothian from one club to another – but not if you're:

1. A woman
2. A radioactive leper.

SAWNEY BEAN

Now people in Ayrshire are as fond of an undetermined meat product as the rest of the country, but the activities of one family in the county took it too far. When rumours began to spread about unseemly events, no one batted an eyelid. But they were wrong not to bat, because a family led by Sawney Bean were cannibals. They'd hit passers-by on the head and then eat them. They'd surprise travellers down the coast and eat them. People enjoying a sunny day on the beach would find their repose rudely interrupted by being gobbled up. It wasn't good for the tourism industry and so something had to be done, and by following the trail of gnawed bones the family Bean was captured and given a roasting. After this telling off, they were set on fire.

It later emerged that the whole thing might have been invented in the Seventeen Oatcakes by an English writer

* Not very welcome.

hoping to give Scots a bad name, but we don't need any help, thanks all the same!

MARY, QUEEN OF SCOTS

What can be said about Mary, Queen of Scots that hasn't been said before? She was a wise and regal monarch whose stable government ensured a steady period of governance without scandal or revolt. Like the axe that cleaved her head from her shoulders, she divides opinion. Was she a tartar or a martyr? A naïve or a nyaff? A queen or a has-been? A wit or a should probably stop there?

As a child of not many years, Mary had been packed off to marry the French King, who was called The Dauphin, hilariously confused with Dolphin for almost 500 years. He did not live long and when he went belly-up, Mary was left an unmerry widow. She returned to Scotland after thirteen years away, which was unlucky for some – i.e. her.

A Catholic woman monarch arriving in the middle of the Protestant Reformation was a recipe for trouble. John Knox, who used to hilariously joke about going to the school of Hard Knox, was apoplectic, aggrieved, appalled, antagonised and aghast. And that's just the As – wait until you heard him on the Fs. He wrote a pamphlet in the days when pamphlets were the social media channel of choice. Pamphlet – a word that, the more you say it, the more it sounds funny. Pamphlet. Pamphlet. Try it. Pamphlet. Told you.

They say you can't judge a book by its cover, but you *can* judge a pamphlet by its title. Knox's was entitled *The First*

Blast of the Trumpet against the Monstrous Regiment of Women. *Cosmopolitan*, *Red* and *Marie Claire* all strangely failed to serialise it, although the *Daily Mail* thought it good, but only if they could illustrate with a picture of Mary, Queen of Scots getting out of a carriage wearing a short skirt.

His tome railed against half the population who, to a woman, thought he would get his comeuppance when he got home. He was married – to a woman – and risked his parables getting chapped between two heavyweight prayer books. As far as we know, this wasn't done, as he had five children.

Around this time, Mary travelled around Scotland a lot in a vain attempt to avoid being shouted at by Foxy Knoxy. It was clear that he hated the Scots Queen. Or did he? Was there something about Mary? Did he secretly fancy her and concoct a fantasy scenario whereby his bearded, gruff, Presbyterian self would be as like a Greek god to Aphrodite and she'd beckon him into her boudoir for the Greek equivalent of *beaucoup d'amour dans une grand numbre des positiones*? We'll never know. It's unlikely, but people said Wales would never get to a major football championship again and look at them.*

Mary had bad luck with the men in her love life. When she returned to Scotland, she had got married to the dashing Lord Darnley, so described as he was often seen dashing into the bedrooms of young women who

* In 2016 they did, to the European Championships in France. The only British Isles team not to attend was Scotland. We were busy washing our hair.

weren't his wife. He was vain, egocentric, foolish, violent, nasty and a drunkard. But apart from that: a catch. He was fertile, perhaps too fertile, but in those days, that was seen as a good thing. Royal dynasties relied on a constant supply of love action and Darnley was up for that, if not in the right place.

He was eventually blown up and stabbed to death. Not the way he planned to go, but who did? That was two husbands down for her. She completed the hat-trick by marrying the Earl of Bothwell, who was thought responsible for offing Darnley. These guys did a lot of editing on their love-match profiles.

Now, when Mary was queen there was actually some peace from the usual Scotland vs England fighting. As her mum was French, she had brought over some of her countrymen. Having French people in Scotland added much culture. Scots would find themselves shrugging more and they developed a fondness for long and thin bits of bread. Some dabbled in existentialism, but found it a bit too depressing – certainly for those living in Saltcoats, who didn't need any French philosophers informing them of the bleakness of human existence. But these French were Catholics. And Mary was one too. And John Knox didn't like Catholics. And the Protestant English queen, Queen Elizabeth One, didn't like them either. The Protestant Scots were torn. Their natural enemy, England, now looked to be on their side. Their eyes went crossed trying to work out who to dislike.

There was much intrigue and these Scots eventually thought they'd better do something about Mary* and so she was usurped from the throne and chased off. She went to England, where she was sure she'd get a warm welcome from her cousin Queen Liz. You know what they say about it being better to travel in hope than arrive in disappointment? It's bad enough having your head chopped off, but if it's done on the orders of your cousin who has had you cooped up for nineteen years it's really not great. And when the chopping is done badly, and there's a lot more hacking and hewing than necessary, it can be downright unpleasant. So it was with our Mary.

The executioner's hood either slipped down over his eyes at the crucial moment, he was nervous with everyone watching (not all men can do it while being watched), or he got distracted by pondering what to have for tea. Whatever happened, when he brought down the heavy axe, he did well to at least hit the prostate figure before him. He didn't cut his own legs off, so that's also something in his favour. He didn't kill the Scottish Queen in one fell swoop – oh no. He had to quickly regain his poise and have another go. In golfer's parlance, it was three off the tee by that point. Eventually, proud Mary was in more bits than when she came into the world. Her head was held up as proof she was dead and, just at that minute, her lips

* Keen-eyed readers will notice this second reference to the gross-out movie comedy starring Cameron Diaz. That's a £5 bet secured that such an amount of mentions could be made in a Scottish history book.

moved and those close by swore she whispered, 'Oh ya' – proving that despite all the trappings of France, she was definitely Scottish.

MORAY, MAR AND MORTON

Not an alliterative firm of lawyers but the Earls of Moray, Mar and Morton. These men were all regents, which meant they got to rule the country but wouldn't get to call themselves king or wear ermine. Some of them defied this edict and secretly wore ermine underpants under their puffed-out breeches.

They had mixed fortunes – sudden death mixed with more sudden death.

Moray was shot in the relatively peaceful town of Linlithgow, becoming the first person to be assassinated by a firearm. Not just in Linlithgow, but the world. It's not a great claim to fame, but it still counts. Mar died after allegedly being poisoned by his successor: the Earl of Morton. It's not something they teach at the Harvard Business School, but it certainly worked in the Sixteenth Century Oatcake.

Morton has his own claim to fame, as he introduced the guillotine to Scotland. This was a wooden structure with two towers, in between which a very sharp metal blade was suspended. The blade was released and it fell downwards onto the soon-to-be-departed person's neck. It's similar to those things you can buy from a catalogue that will chop up carrots, and indeed when the guillotine was first brought in it was demonstrated to watching punters by putting a carrot into the slot. (This was stopped by the Vegan Society, who thought it cruel to carrots who deserved to see out the rest of their lives rotting to black at the bottom of the vegetable rack.)

Morton wanted to send a strong message to convicted criminals. (Unconvicted criminals were not guillotined, as they had gotten away with it.) In one of those ironic twists of history, Morton got his own head chopped off by his own innovation – a very extreme form of product testing. They do say that if you're a Ford car salesman you should drive a Ford, after all.

With Moray, Mar and Morton out of the way, it was time for a king. Another king called James.

12 KING JAMES SIX

OR

LOCK UP YOUR DAUGHTERS (IF THEY'RE WITCHES)

Mary's son, Prince James Six, became King James Six on her removal from being a queen. He dribbled and made no sense when he talked and was immediately elected as a sports commentator on talk radio, until it was realised he was 13 months old.

Now, poor Wee James did not have an idyllic childhood, being taken at an early age from his mother in case he caught her Catholicism. He was given a very strict upbringing, being told in no uncertain terms what was right (Protestantism) from wrong (Catholicism). In time James grew up and got to sit on the throne as a proper king. He was regarded as a good king, though not by the women he had tortured and burnt as witches. They rated him 'Below Average' on KingAdvisor.

Witches around this time were the scourge of honest, hardworking subjects. They were the immigrants/dole scroungers/single mothers/asylum seekers/travellers/Mods and Rockers/illegal ravers/young people/refugees/street charity collectors/mobile phone salesmen of the time. You could blame them for anything! Bad sea harvest? Witches did that. Poor harvest? Witches. Your team lost a last-minute penalty? Well that'll be the witches, then. Eventually the witches had enough of this and split to the four points of the compass, where some turned to good and others to bad, living in castles and training flying monkeys to do their bidding.

Although not the worst Stuart* king, James was deemed 'the wisest fool in Christendom'. He wasn't sure how to take this and consulted the cleverest moron in Sikhism and the thickest genius in Judaism, but they were none the wiser either. He famously said, 'No bishop, no king', which meant chess games were rendered useless.

But bigger things were about to happen. In Sixteen Oatcake, James got the news he'd been waiting for: Good Queen Bess was now Good Queen Dead. Queen Elizabeth One of England was no more and James was her successor. For our James, opportunity was knocking. He expressed great sadness at the thought of leaving Scotland, while hurriedly packing his bags and heading south. As he jumped up onto his horse, he said he would miss the old place and would 'rule Scotland by pen'. Sheep farmers praised this method of establishing authority until they realised it was the writing type of pen. They went back to traipsing around the soggy, heathery hills muttering about the bureaucracy of Europe.

After his coronation in London, James was now King James Six of Scotland and One of England. Before this 'Union of the Crowns', James had done something that was unusual: he didn't start a war between Scotland and England. What kind of king was that? One who wanted to die in his bed an old man? Pah! That's not good for dramatic history purposes.

* James' mother Mary, Queen of Scots had changed the spelling as she thought the original 'Stewart' a bit too common, while 'Stuart' was more French and therefore more chic.

He did wage a campaign against smoking which, four centuries later, shows real results. He also did do one thing that led to a little bit of Trouble later: he sent people to live in Ireland. Now, it might have missed old Jamesie, but there were folk already living there who weren't too pleased with this influx of settlers and there was some fighting, to be sure.

Someone else who wasn't best pleased with our King Jimbo was Guy Fawkes, who plotted to blow up the Houses of Parliament with gunpowder. He was caught and bad things happened to him, but his name echoed down the centuries with people doing daft things 'For Fawkes' Sake'. And at least he's remembered, unlike the other conspirators, namely er, him that was there and that other guy, you know the one. With the beard. Tall lad.

THE BIBLE

In Sixteen Oatcake, The King James Bible came out, published by The King James. It was in English and, with a three-for-two offer on it, sold like hot cross buns at Easter. Punters flocked to find out what happened to the heroes, God and his Son, although some thought the Holy Ghost took away from the central narrative and also gave them the heebie-jeebies (heebie-jeebies). Some readers ignored the spoiler warnings* and felt a bit disappointed. However, if you gave it less than five stars men would come round with thumbscrews and ask you to reconsider.

* Jesus dies.

Despite the accessibility offered, very few people read the Bible all the way through. (It's a bit like the user agreement when signing up to a new social media thing – although if you miss the small print you might lose copyright on your photographs, rather than losing your soul in everlasting fires.) Those that got bored used the pages with small pieces of wood to light their fires in the morning. They were the first kindle users …

CHARLES ONE

In the usual way, King Charles One became king when his dad James Six and One died, in Sixteen Oatcake. Charles made the major mistake of being arrogant, vain and self-obsessed. If he'd appeared in a reality TV show he might have earned a decent living opening nightclubs. But he was a king, and instead made life hard for those coming into contact with him.

He interfered in the running of the Church. He thought it should be 'Our father who art in heaven', while the Church leaders thought it should be 'Our father who *are* in heaven', which was grammatically incorrect and this drove Charles to the edge of rage, him being a keen grammar fan who, amongst other things, hated ending sentences with prepositions like 'to'.

One of his actions was to fiddle with – and there's no other way to put this, as it was the term used to describe them – the Lords of Erection. They had been given land formerly belonging to the Church and when the king tried to take away these lands they visibly stiffened.*

* When will they bring back the Carry On films?

The common peasants weren't too chuffed with King Jim One either. In Edinburgh, when a new prayer book was unveiled the congregation flung stools at the minister. Poo-eee! Oh no, it's okay, it wasn't a dirty protest. It was just the stools people sit on. Phew! The minister was certainly glad. A broken nose, cut eye and fractured skull could have been *much* worse. You have to remember that non-bio washing powders were not invented by a Scotsperson yet.

13 CIVIL WAR

OR

KING CHARLIE AND THE COVENANTING FACTORY

Following the stool-throwing, there was much tumult and unrest. In Edinburgh a committee called the Tables was formed. It was headed by a Chair, and the Chair and Tables would sit for hours in the esteemed rooms of Edinburgh, scraping away on the wooden floors until the downstairs neighbours told them to stop.

Then one day, a momentous event took place that would echo down the centuries: the signing of the National Covenant in Greyfriars Kirk (Kirk) in Edinburgh, witnessed by a small white dog that was to achieve immortality later on. After signing the Covenant (the document that they signed), these 'Covenanters' roamed the country to rant, roar, greet, yell, yelp, harangue, haver and yammer away at any poor soul they came across. They had fire in their bellies and boy were you going to hear about it, whether you wanted to or not.

The Covenanters were the ravers of their era, organising secret meet-ups around the country under the eyes of the watchful authorities. While the late Twentieth Century Oatcake ravers preached 'Es are good'* their earlier counterparts preached 'He is good'. He being God. And, oh, did they spread His Word(s). Like overzealous charity chuggers, their attempts at persuasion were not welcomed 100 per cent. People would see them up ahead and suddenly become interested in that tree over there, or that cloud that looked like a goat and attempt to sneak past unobserved.

* Don't know why they singled out that letter, they're all pretty good. Apart from Q, if you're playing Scrabble.

But tumult and unrest weren't enough to go on, and in Sixteen Thirty Oatcake the clouds darkened (it *was* summer) and minds started to turn towards fighting and war. Around this time, Scottish troops were coming home after fighting abroad. They couldn't believe their luck when they found there was a chance of a scrap and, for novelty's sake, a religious one. The 'Thou shalt not kill' part of the old Bible was quietly pushed aside, a bit like that purple lettuce you get served with your lasagne. A lot of the king's men met the Covenanting Army at Berwick and ran around asking everyone to keep calm and to carry on, in what was known as the Pacification of Berwick. Would it last, though?

IT'S MORE WAR!

No.

Things boiled over and a 'civil war' broke out. Everyone desired to be the best at complimenting each other on their armour or where they got their spurs done. Then they realised this was boring and started plunging pikes into each other's bodies. In England there were two sides: the Roundheads and the Cavaliers. The Roundheads were fighting to have a Parliament free of too much royal interference and the Cavaliers weren't.

In Scotland, people didn't know what to do: should they fight the king or the Covenanters? In the end, some did both. The Marquee of Montrose was on the Covenanter side and then switched to supporting King Charlie. Montrose went on a scenic tour of Scotland, visiting many of the places where Mary, Queen of Scots stayed in an attempt to avoid being shouted at by John Knox, and he also fitted in some fighting. He took Aberdeen, Dundee, Glasgow and Perth, but lost at Philiphaugh.*

When King Charles was captured by the Covenanters in Sixteen Forty Oatcake, Montrose cursed switching sides as he was on the losing one at the time. He was forced out of the country and fled to a cold and distant land. No, not Pittenweem: Norway.

THE KING IS DEAD, HERE'S ANOTHER ONE

In Sixteen Forty Oatcake, King Charles One followed his grandmother to the chopping block. It is the sort of family tradition you do not want to establish. Always being the ones who have to cook for everyone at Christmas is one thing, this was another. In his place came a man called Oliver Cromwell, who was cruel and unjust *or* a fearless and wise proponent of parliamentary democracy. It's not for us to say which, as we don't know what proponent means. It sounds like opponent so could be a bad thing?

Anyway.

The dead King Charles One was followed by the living King Charles Two. A type of dog or 'spaniel' was named after him, due to his penchant for long curly hair and peeing up lamp posts.

* No idea.

MONTROSE IS BACK!

In Sixteen Fifty Oatcake, the bold Marquee of Montrose returned to the fray, but was unable to repeat his successes. He fell on bad times and wandered the Highlands hungry and alone; so hungry he was reduced – literally – to eating his gloves. This finger buffet wasn't enough to sustain him and he sought shelter in a castle owned by a man called Neil MacLeod, who showed him a lack of the famed traditional Highland hospitality by shopping him to the authorities when he found there was a substantial reward available. Montrose was promptly captured, barely having time to give Neil MacLeod one star on TripAdvisor before being hanged. This killed him, but his legend lives on and echoes down the centuries.

OLIVER CROMWELL'S ARMY

Around this time, the Covenanters decided to side with the king. Cromwell wasn't happy with this – oh no. He invaded Scotland and did bad things, but the Scots got their revenge by him having to be in Scotland for a lengthy time. 'That'll teach him,' they said (to themselves, as Cromwell had good hearing and a bad temper).

Oliver's New Model Army (he liked to upgrade each year) defeated the Scottish troops at Dunbar in Sixteen Fifty Oatcake. The Scottish Army had taken up a good position and Cromwell thought he needed a miracle in order to win. He didn't need a miracle. He was fighting the Scots. Who left their good position for a bad one. Cromwell couldn't believe his luck.

Olly was free to advance into Scotland and he incurred the wrath of Historic Scotland by blasting their abbeys and gift shops with bloody big cannons. He tried to make it up to them by taking out a Lifetime Membership subscription, but things were fraught between them for a long time afterwards.

The Scots swithered about what to do, then a bright spark in the strategic planning team thought they should do the traditional thing and lose to an English army, and so King Charles Two ordered his men to march to battle at Worcester in England, as they hadn't gotten beaten there before. They couldn't say this after the inevitable defeat in Sixteen Fifty Oatcake.

After this loss, Charles legged it into exile and spent some time wandering about Europe. But God loves a trier and in Sixteen Sixty Oatcake Cromwell died and Charles was 'restored' to the throne. Showing terrific imagination, this event was known as the 'Restoration'.

During his period in charge Charlie boy told the Covenanters that he was only joking when he'd signed up with them and that he was going to have a proper old church, like his father and grandfather. The bishops were back! The Covenanters were harried and hunted and, to give an idea of what it was like, this period was known as 'The Killing Time'. Hundreds of Covenanters were imprisoned in Greyfriars Cemetery, which saved a lot of time, as a lot of them died.

Due to his hedonistic lifestyle, King Charles became known as the 'Merry Monarch'. The Merry Monarch became Not Quite So Merry when he died in Sixteen Eighty Oatcake.

14 ANOTHER KING MESS

OR

JAMES OH OH SEVEN

With the king's death, everyone looked around: what to do? Elect a president? Vote in a prime minister? Form a governing collective on a democratic basis of equal representation of the population's demographic?

In the end they went for getting a king in. Well, it was traditional after all. He was King James Seven and Two, which sounds like a golf score. Being a Stuart king, the odds were always going to be stacked against him and he was thrown off the throne. The Historic England sign clearly stated, 'Do Not Sit On The Thrones'. Them's the rules.

Being a Catholic king, he was understandably sympathetic to others who were also Catholics – but sympathy got you nowhere in these days. When told he was being ousted, he said, 'Oh yeah, the day I get ousted I'm a Dutchman.' This was unfortunate, as he was replaced by a Dutchman: King William of Orange. King Willy fitted the bill for being a king of the time in Britain: he was a Protestant. The fact he wasn't British but a foreign person from the Netherlands was not brought up in polite conversation. He never set foot in Scotland – he'd been well briefed.

In the Highlands, the locals (known as 'Highlanders' because of where they lived) were not hugely impressed by King James Seven and Two being given his marching orders. They took action, furiously scribbling letters to the *Sunday Post* (and sending off for the promotional muskets). As James's name in Latin is Jacobus, these supporters were known as Jacobites, in the same way that fans of German prisoner-of-war camps are known as Stalagtites.* These Jacobites rebelled

* They can't all be zingers.

and had a few rebellions. This gave them the opportunity to have a war with parts of England (and Scotland).

BONNIE DUNDEE

Bonnie Dundee. You don't hear these two words together often and that's a shame, as the city has a beautiful location, looking across the silvery River Tay to the soft hills of Fife and up the same silvery River Tay towards Perth. Wait a minute, it's not the city, it's a person. Let me look him up. Seems he was a man also known as 'Bloody Clavers'. That's the problem with fame, some love you, some hate you, there's no middle ground.

Bonnie/Bloody was officially called Lord Claverhouse, who ordered his troops to Killiecrankie. Unfortunately, some of his men misheard and attempted to Kill-A-Krankie, but as the pantomime-appearing duo had not been invented yet, they couldn't be found. Instead they marched to Killiecrankie, a place near Perth, and had a battle with the forces of the government. It didn't go well. Bloody Clavers became Deady Clavers.

During the battle, a soldier decided that running away was the better form of cowardice and he leapt over a gorge at the River Garry near to the battle's visitor centre. (Historic Scotland could never be accused of being tardy.) The area became known as The Soldier's Leap. His fate is not known, but as it's not called The Soldier's Fall into the Rocks Below, we can assume he did okay.

GLEN COE MASSACRE

Highland hospitality is renowned the world over. You turn up at a Highlander's house and they'll put you up for the night, feed and water you, and so on. If you're nice, they'll let you see their Runrig albums. If you're not, they'll play them.*

In the late Sixteen Oatcakes, a party of government troops turned up at Glen Coe. (Here is an appropriate place to discuss the correct spelling of Glencoe: Glen Coe is different from Glencoe in that it has a space between the words. You're welcome!) Now these troops were mainly from Clan Campbell and they were staying with their time-served enemies: the MacDonalds. The troops were well looked after, but after two weeks of hospitality, early one morning they got up and, rather than write a nice thank-you letter, murdered their hosts.

Now, we've all left negative reviews, but that is going way too far. You can't just kill people you don't like. Well, it turned out you can if you're the baddies. It was part of a conspiracy by the government to teach some Highlanders a lesson for not submitting their paperwork in time. A lesson for anyone prevaricating on that change of address notification to the council. Luckily, the incident spelled the end of any bad times in the Highlands and everyone worked out their differences in an amiable and amicable way.**

* Only joking.

** Of course it didn't – we've not had Culloden yet.

ROBBING ROY

To some, Rob Roy 'Rob Roy' MacGregor was a bandit and to others he was a bandit, but a bandit who gave them the proceeds of his banditry. This made him a 'folk hero'. It's a fine line between banditry and folk heroitry and MacGregor was happy to tread it. There are many myths and legends that surround MacGregor, so many that the writer of this book couldn't be bothered to write them all down. But there are a lot.

ROBINSON'S BARELY WATERED

Robinson Crusoe, who starred in an eponymous book called *Robinson Crusoe*, was a man isolated, cut off from the civilised world, desperate for intelligent human company he could openly converse with. So, he left Fife and became a sailor. Unfortunately for him, he fell out with the crew and rather than be given a written warning they taunted him for weeks. Eventually he cried out, 'Leave me alone!' So he was deposited on an deserted island on his ownsome. He ate driftwood and made a home out of fish. Or it may have been the other way around. It was a long time ago.

Crusoe wore ragged clothes as when he'd sent his to the launderette he gave the wrong desert island as the return address. Every Friday he was visited by a man who, luckily, was called Man Friday. Crusoe dreamed of a Woman Friday, but she never showed up. Despite his many, many years of solitude, he survived and returned to civilisation.

On his arrival he was asked by Kirsty Young about his life and what songs he really liked.

EDINBURGH

Edinburgh's past is more exciting than you might think at first glance. A staid, worthy city of solid buildings and even more solid foodstuffs, it has long been the capital of Scotland. There is a famous expression that represents the perceived unwelcoming nature of the citizens, 'You wouldn't be rude enough to turn up here announced expecting to have your tea at our expense, are you?'

The fact Edinburgh is Scotland's major tourist destination shows how false this expression is and the city ranks high in the list of top places in the Lothians to visit. Centuries ago, it just ranked. People would utter French words before tipping their rubbish down in front of bemused citizens – a service now carried out in fine dining restaurants. Around this time Edinburgh was called 'Auld Reekie', a name that came after a prolonged committee brainstorming session that saw 'Cauld Reekie' pipped at the post and 'Bauld Reekie' a distant third. The latter was suggested by members of the Bauld family from Corstorphine, who have to be admired for their audacity, though why they wanted to highlight their lack of head hair to the world is not known.

BANKS

In the late Sixteen Oatcakes a Scotsperson invented banking. Yes, a system whereby all that lovely money that's yours that you then pay someone to keep for you? You're welcome. Getting charged for receiving a letter telling you that you owe this bank money? You're very much welcome! Having to see your hospital closed because the banks spent all their money – and all the country's money, too? Oops sorry about that!

Around this time, Scots were proud of their new bank. It was given a fiendishly inventive name. It was called the 'Bank of Scotland'. But this name was part of the attraction: nothing too fancy, a sensible place to put your hard-earned cash away for a rainy day.*

Now Scots are renowned for being naturally reticent to embrace new ideas. Just look at how long it took the country to adopt a free holiday at Christmas. They can be a canny and cautious lot; some might say it's the hallmark of a sensible nation. Having this attitude means that Scots would never get involved in a get-rich-quick scheme that promised untold riches without any real graft having to be done – would they?**

DARIEN SCHEME

Economists, historians and people who look up Wikipedia have struggled to succinctly sum up the Darien Scheme. Most have settled on: disaster. A total '******* ****_**' would also suffice.

* Or Monday, Tuesday, Wednesday, Thursday, Friday, Saturday, Sunday, as we call them.

** Yes, they would.

The plan was to start a colony in Panama that would allow trade to burgeon. Burgeoning trade was seen as 'a good thing' for the economy and, with the added incentive of getting first dibs on the area's riches, Scots were excited about their first colony. Riches would unfold, it'd be great! They went to bed early, like children on Christmas Eve excited about Santa coming to visit. Those proposing the idea caught the imagination of the population of Scotland, who rushed to invest in this gilt-edged scheme. The country funded five boats to venture to the colony: *Titanic*, *Lusitania*, *Marie Celeste*, *Mary Rose* and *Exxon Valdes*. What could go wrong?*

Darien was hot and humid, but the Scots had thoughtfully packed woolly jumpers 'just in case'. There was no clean water. It was smelly and full of annoying pests. Not backpackers intent on having a 'life experience' before settling as financial consultants as they hadn't been invented yet, these were insect bugs. There were more creepy crawlies than in a one-star guest house duvet. You'd think people from Scotland would be used to swatting small insects, having come from the Land of the Midge, but no, this was a different kettle of fish. Speaking of fish, the colonists never mastered the art of catching this freely available nutritious food, instead eating mouldy old dough.

It would have made a decent reality celebrity TV show, but with real people it wasn't good. It started badly and ended worse. Many people died and much money was lost. Scots would never again get involved in an adventure in

* Everything. Oops, belated spoiler alert!

South America.* It didn't help that the Dutch King Willy was against the idea and did whatever he could to scupper the plans. This fed resentment in Scotland which would normally result in one thing: a war against England. But times were different and, more importantly, Scotland was cash poor. A little thing called the Act of Union was about to take place which would echo down the centuries.

ACT OF UNION

Scotland was without money, but its southern neighbour had money and so was happy to help out. But there was a catch. It insisted on political and economic union. The bank only wants your house! But after much gnashing and wailing of teeth – and large financial bribes – in Seventeen Oatcake Scotland joined with England. They would have a joint flag and each country would support the other in any international sporting tournament.**

Robert the Bruce and William Wallace turned in their graves, in Wallace's case: graves. Opinion was divided amongst Scots: some were happy, but some were absolutely raging, smashing up the crockery and clutching their fists, looking up at the sky and screaming 'Why?' Many were gutted because this union meant there'd be no more wars. Was this what their ancestors had died needlessly for – peace?

* They did. See World Cup, Argentina, 1978.
** Didn't last long.

15 BONNIE PRINCE CHARLIE

OR

THEY THINK IT'S HANOVER

In Seventeen Oatcake, the Queen Anne who had overseen the Union died from overwork – those dressing tables don't varnish themselves. European family trees were scoured, branch by branch, until a suitable candidate could be found. Eventually a short list was created, interviews were held and one was selected. He made his way to London, where he was exuberantly greeted by cries of 'Who's this geezer?', 'Eh?' and 'Is there a twenty-eight-day return policy?'

The personal credentials required on the job description had said, 'Protestant', and that's what they got. King George One was fat, in his forties and couldn't speak a word of English. In Scotland, the population were bemused, bothered and bewildered. The Catholic Scots were sad, seething, and said as soon as the pub was closed they were going to do something about it. When they woke up hung-over they knew they'd agreed to do something but couldn't remember what it was. Three days later, they were walking along the street when, like a bolt out of the blue, they remembered. They were to have a rebellion!

So, in Seventeen Oatcake a rebellion was duly had. The Jacobites did get to fight in England, though they suffered an away defeat in Preston, followed by a home defeat at Sheriffmuir in Perthshire. Muttering about the shocking refereeing decisions, they trudged home – those that weren't dead, that is. But the Jacobites weren't finished. Oh no.

BONNIE PRINCE CHARLIE (BPC)

Charles Edward Louis Philip Casimir John Paul George Ringo Fleegle Bingo Drooper Snork Stuart was born in Seventeen Oatcake and, due to his name, spent much of his early life filling in forms. He was called many other things: 'Bonnie Prince Charlie', 'The King O'er the Water', 'The Young Pretender', 'The Young Chevalier', and 'That Absolute **** of a Man'. No person in Scottish history was the cause of so much grief as he. We're talking worse than Berti Vogts.* He came, he saw, he utterly failed.

BPC wanted to reclaim the British throne for his dad, who was known as 'The Great Pretender'. When asked in coffee houses, he would wearily reply, 'Yes. I'm The Great Pretender, oo-oo-oo.' So, in order to cheer up his pa, BPC decided to go to Scotland, win the crown, restore the Catholic and Stuart monarchy and relax, having got the job done. Probably get a bike for Christmas as a reward.

When he sailed into Scotland, he was met by some Jacobites. He stepped ashore and thanked them for coming, asked if they lived locally and sniffed the smell of new paint. It should be said that some of his welcoming party weren't too welcoming, telling him to go home. Showing his effortless command of the language of the country into which he arrived, BPC replied, 'I am come home.'

Pleasantries out of the way, he asked where the main army was. His welcomers looked around, scratching their

* Only Scotland could get a German football manager who brought chaos and disorganisation.

beards. Some whistled, others found something really interesting to look at over there, and eventually the hairiest Highlander (by law, how clan chieftains are chosen) told him that this *was* the main army. BPC turned quietly round, jumped into the water and started swimming for his ship and had to be hauled back to fulfil his destiny that would echo down the centuries.

He was reassured that there were loads of loyal followers who had to return library books that day and would soon join them on the march to victory. With this news and a song in their heart (Talking Heads' 'We're on the Road to Nowhere') they marched off to glory or death.*

Without going into unnecessarily researched detail BPC gloriously captured Scotland, but like a gambler who doesn't know when to fold or when to walk away, he advanced into England. With his merry band of hairy Highlanders, they got as far as Derby. With London only a short distance away, BPC's commanders decided 'Nah', and turned about, believing a large army stood in the way of the tourist hotspots of the British capital. It was a cruel blow, BPC was seeing his dreams dashed in front of his eyes. He'd been occupied with thoughts of London. On the way down, he'd hummed and hawed over what colour cape to wear on his imminent triumphant entrance. He was going to go with the blue. His fateful decision (to retreat, not to pick the blue cape) was to have bad consequences for many of his followers.

* Not the first one. Belated spoiler alert!

With his trusty band of warriors, BPC headed back north. The government were not going to let them just quietly return home. Oh no. They met near the visitor centre at Culloden, outside Inverness, where the kind of crushing defeat normally suffered by the hopes of Scotland football fans was dished out. The battle was over in less than an hour. The Jacobite soldiers were tired and hungry, but this soon became a passing concern. They were hit by musket fire, cannon fire and, if they survived that, they risked being stabbed by very pointy bayonets. The Hanoverian Army didn't just rub salt into the wounds of the injured but also shoved those pointy bayonets.

By this point, for many on the battlefield the novelty of BPC had definitely worn off. He legged it as fast as he could from the battlefield. One of his generals shouted after him, 'Run, you Italian coward!', which was unfair as the horse wasn't Italian and hadn't much choice in where it was steered.

Dressed as a woman, and with a woman dressed as a woman called Flora MacDonald, he toured the west Highlands as the Laddie Boys, in a forerunner of popular tartan duo, Fran and Anna. Eventually he'd gotten all the souvenirs he wanted and returned to Italy. The double act with Flora missed a great opportunity at the Edinburgh Fringe, where it would definitely have received five stars from *The Scotsman*.

Back in Italy, Bonnie Prince Charlie soon became Not So Bonnie Fattie Boom-Boom Prince Charlie, as he toured the bars telling anyone who wasn't quick enough that 'I coulda been a contender'. He never returned to sobriety or Scotland again.

The victorious government took no chances and made sure there were to be no more uprisings. They set up forts and roads and forbade anyone to wear tartan. This left shop owners in Edinburgh's Royal Mile bereft, but it didn't end there. Gaelic was also banned, spelling bad news for road sign painters, who had to redo them all into only English. Bagpipes were banned and thousands were up in arms. 'Why didn't we do this ages ago?' they wailed, thinking of the sleep they'd now be getting. While it might not sound too bad, for very many of those in the Highlands it would lead to Very Bad Things.

16 THE ENLIGHTENMEN

OR

WATT WAS THE NAME OF THE MAN WHO INVENTED THE STEAM CONDENSER?

It's said that not much happens very quickly in Edinburgh – a thesis which has some validity, as it has a New Town which is over 200 years old. Plans for a Brand Spanking New Town are awaiting council approval and have been since the 1950s.

In the Eighteenth Century Oatcake, the city became the centre of the Scottish Enlightenment, which was ironic as, amongst those high-brow,* high-brained, high-trousered participants, no one had thought to invent electric lighting and so they had to scrabble about in the dark.

The finest minds gathered, all of them to become household names:

David 'Thinker' Hume
Adam 'Money' Smith
James 'The Rock' Hutton
Robert 'Son of William' Adam
Joseph 'The Chemist' Black
James 'Power' Watt

The latter was the source of a particularly amusing bon mot (bon mot) that did the dinner party table rounds. A guest would ask quietly to a dining neighbour, 'What was the name of the man who invented the steam condenser?'

'Watt,' would be the reply.

The questioner would whisper a little bit louder, '*What* was the name of the man who invented the steam condenser?'

The answerer would come back, 'Watt!'

* Facial hair, like smallpox, was out of control back then

And on it would go, each one losing their temper and, ironically, blowing off steam at being duped by such a hilarious joke. (Around this time, people prayed for a Scotsperson to invent television.)

The Enlighteners would talk about anything and everything: politics, philosophy, science, economics, medicine, geology, how to chat up girls while being a nerd and, in their way, shaped the future destiny of the world. They invented the Industrial Revolution and influenced the American Revolution. So you know who to blame.

THE PORTEOUS MOB

One incident that is still written about today (even if it is just in this book) took place in Edinburgh in Seventeen Thirty Oatcake. A man named Captain Porteous was lynched and hanged from a pole for something he did, by what became known as the Porteous Mob.* Around this time, things were different. Nowadays, no one would have a bit of rope handy. Do you have a length of rope able to hang a man? Didn't think so. And that is a good thing.

BURKE AND HARE

Of all the double acts to cause misery to the Scottish population over the centuries: plague and pestilence, Jimmy and Ian Krankie, Burke and Hare – it is difficult to pin down the worst, but the latter have a unique claim to

* *Similar to a flash mob, but with a scaffold.*

infamy. This pair of Irish rogues did not really dig up stiffs and wheel them off to the dissection table at Edinburgh University's medical school (motto: 'You'll have had your life'). Instead, they saved themselves a lot of digging work by just bumping off whoever was handy. Once dead, the poor souls were taken to Cash for Cadavers and Burke and Hare went off for a wee swally with the proceeds.

Eventually they were arrested. Hare quickly dobbed in his partner and Burke was duly hanged in front of thousands in Edinburgh's Grassmarket in Eighteen Oatcake. Edinburghers squeezed into any available viewing spot to see a nasty man asphyxiated on the end of a rope. Nowadays they jostle to watch a man on a unicycle reciting Hamlet during the Festival. You tell me which is the bigger crime.

ROBERT BURNS

Robert Burns is Scotland's greatest poet. He had an eye for the ladies and, judging by the subsequent family trees, something else for them too. He was termed the 'Ploughman Poet' for his love of a sturdy meal of cheese, pickled onion, pickled apple and pickle. This was apt as food was important to Burns. Without it he would have died much earlier than he did.

Burns Suppers were invented (by Scotspersons, of course) to commemorate his memory, whereby a haggis (consisting of – best to look away if you're vegan – oatmeal, onion, small pieces of animals, barley, salt, spices, all served up inside a bag made of a sheep stomach) is the centrepiece. You do wonder what they would have served if they didn't like him.

In a Burns Supper, the haggis has its guts ploughed open by a great big knife and while Scots are a (mostly) peaceful race it's understandable if people think otherwise if, at our most high-profile mealtime, we stab the main course.

As well as eating, fornicating and writing poems, our Robert wrote songs and letters. He was a busy man. Sadly, there was no arts council funding available and he had to also work at the same time. Ploughing a field was not too conducive to creative writing, as the pen was bumped all over the place. In the evenings, with his wife, children and farm animals abed, he would sit by the dim glow of a candle and try to work out what he'd written. This is why, to a modern audience, some of the words aren't well known – he didn't know what the hell they were either. In this way, he wrote poems and songs that echo down the centuries, such as 'To a Mouse', 'To a Louse' and others that don't rhyme with 'ouse'.

Burns became a legend. If he was alive today, not only would he be very old but he would get laughed at for wearing those breeches. How exactly did they go to the toilet?

SMOKIN'!

For many years Glasgow was a small town by the River Clyde and it slowly developed into a bigger town, still by the River Clyde. As it grew, it had been visited by Mary, Queen of Scots, who stayed there in an attempt to avoid being shouted at by John Knox.

Things in the city were rolling along fine until someone had the idea of becoming 'rich'. This concept involved accumulating large amounts of 'money' and 'keeping it'. This 'wealth', as it came to be known, came at a cost, but not for those becoming 'wealthy'. Glasgow's 'Tobacco Lords' got their money by importing 'tobacco' which was harvested by 'slaves'. To anyone with a modern conscience there's a couple of items there that might cause a trembling of the moral barometer. Back then, it was a case of 'tough chuckies' for those at the enslaved end of the work chain. Harsh, but unfair.

Glasgow had spent its ill-gotten gains wisely, only blowing half of it on horse racing and lottery scratch cards. The other half was used to build fine townhouses and fine boulevards named after the once-burgeoning trade:

Jamaica Street
Virginia Street
Coughing Street
Black Phlegm Street

Eventually slavery was abolished. (Some missed the good old days, although no one saying this was an actual slave.) It was thought intolerable to have people working in terrible conditions for no money. So, this was to be replaced by having them work in terrible in conditions for next to no money. But before the Industrial Revolution began, something else had to take place.

THE CLEARANCES

The Clearances saw carpets, beds and furniture all at crazy knocked-down prices. Everything must go! And as their owners were thrown off their land, it did! Landowners had wanted to have a people-free Highlands. They wished to commission paintings of their estates' scenic grandeur, and the humans peppered about the place weren't as aesthetically pleasing as sheep, so off they went.

The Clearances were not welcomed, it has to be said, and there was some uncivil disobedience. These doughty Highlanders weren't going to take it lying down, although this is how they ended up after being knocked down with wooden truncheons. The trouble led to the Battle of the Braes, which saw little actual fighting, just two hills staring menacingly at each saying, 'Hold me back, Margaret.'

Whole communities and family trees were uprooted and given little option but to clear off. They boarded leaky and cramped boats and were transported to Australia, New Zealand, Canada or America. Once they landed in these foreign lands, filled with their wide expanses, unspoilt natural wildernesses, clear spring water, all drenched with that essence of loveliness – the sun – some forgot all about Scotch … Schoat … Skit … whatever that place was they used to call home. (Except for those who died on route in those stinking disease-ridden boats or drowned when they sank – they didn't enjoy the experience quite as much.)

Not all forgot the old country though, naming the settlements they now called home after the places they previously called home. In Canada there was an Aberdeen.

In America, an Aberdeen. In Sierra Leone, an Aberdeen. The original Aberdeen didn't feel special any more and thought about changing its name to The Original (And Best) Aberdeen, but soon sobered up.

Of the thousands who had been forced to leave their homes, many didn't move abroad but to someplace just as exotic: Glasgow. They moved here and other burgeoning cities where a revolution was taking place, on an industrial scale.*

* The Industrial Revolution.

17 THE INDUSTRIAL REVOLUTION

OR

WHEN WILL FLEXI-TIME BE INVENTED?

The Industrial Revolution needed power, to power all the machines that made up the powerful industrial processes. These were big metal things that went 'whumpf' and smaller ones made of wood that went 'swish-swoosh swish-swoosh'. Other machines went 'tweeeeeeeee' and 'gdoink'. Eventually, it was thought they should add some functions to them in addition to the noises so they could start making things.

At first water powered this industry. This water turned big wheels and, in turn, they turned other things and then some other stuff happened and – ta-da! – cotton came out. This was great news for everyone tired of hemp lingerie. But, despite the great advantage of being free, water wasn't enough – it also wasn't wholly efficient as the constant sound of running water meant workers were always rushing off to the toilet.

Mill owners pondered what to do and then were inspired by the smoke issuing from their cigars. Cigars needed combustible materials which produced heat. But their efforts to power their whumpf, swish-swoosh, swish-swoosh, tweeeeeeeee and gdoink machines with smoke didn't work as the children they were using to blow the smoke into the machines were getting lung cancer. This caused much anguish and pain to the mill owners, whose hands got sore writing 'get well soon' cards.

Then someone had another great idea: steam! But there was none around. They went to Iceland, where there was plenty, but the locals insisted on serving fermented shark balls and so they soon left. Another method of creating steam power was needed, and luckily a Scotsperson was around who was able to invent just the thing.

JAMES WATT

His name, as was mentioned earlier for those dogged readers still with us, was Watt, James Watt. He puzzled over what to do until one day in his laboratory he bolted out of his seat and shouted, 'Eureka!' His assistants stared, open mouthed. Watt said to them, 'Eureka! That's what Archimedes shouted when he came up with his invention. I wonder what I'll say when I have mine?' He sat back down and pondered some more. His assistants sighed.

Eventually his pondering paid off and his 'watting machine' became a sure-fire hit, producing clouds of steamy power. This power was used to great effect and, although the workers using it endured long hours of unending, grim, mind-corrupting, sweaty toil, they were compensated by knowing that the man behind it all would end up on a tea towel and in a silly book. Some workers felt this wasn't enough and demanded recompense for their sweaty toil, so factory and mill owners gave them shiny coins – not all of which contained chocolate.

INVENTIONS

Watt was just one of the many Scotsperson inventors who invented pretty much everything. These are just some of the many thousands of things that were invented:*

* Source: tea towel bought on the Royal Mile.

Bicycles
Tricycles
Icicles
Sticky postage stamps
Cheese
Anaesthetic
Clouds
Telephone
Television
Telly Savalas
Geology
American Navy
Swiss Navy
Salvation Army
Penicillin
Electromagnetism
Paraffin
Radar
Rabbits
Rainbows

EXPERIMENTS

It was all very well inventing things, but you had to back them up with precise and scientific experiments. One such experiment was performed by a man who went by the name of Nevil Maskelyne, who was the Astronomer Royale. His reputation had spread and in Paris he was known as the Big Cheese Astronomer Royale.

In Seventeen Seventy Oatcake, he climbed the Scottish mountain Schiehallion (Schiehallion) to measure how big the Earth was. It's probably best not to go into the complicated and time-consuming* mechanics of exactly how he was going to do this, but let's just believe he could.

Once up the hill, he set off a pendulum he'd brought with him but – ah – there was a hiccup. The backwards and forwards movement hypnotised him and Maskelyne now believed onions were tasty apples. On his return to

* Boring.

London to declare the results of his experiment, no one would come near because of his stinky breath. This was a shame as his findings that the Earth was 'Very Big' would have helped science a great deal.

WHISKY

One of Scotland's greatest inventions is whisky. This rich spiky drink that can induce a Scotsperson to show emotion is drunk around the world, although it begs the question – if so popular, why are many malts single?

CANALS

Around this time, Scotland desperately needed to find somewhere to store its shopping trolleys and so a series of canals were built. They were also a good place for barges to slowly move heavy things from one place to another, although they could cause following barges to toot their horns when overtaking going up hills. They were built all over Scotland and this route-canal work was done by men who loved to dig, dig, dig, dig the whole day through. If Twitter was around at the time they would have used the hashtag 'luvdiggin'.

PENICILLIN

Scotspersons have always been known as great medical practitioners. You only have to think of Dr Finlay, Dr Strangelove and Dr Who to realise research should play a key part in any book that has the word 'history' in its title. One of the most important items invented – certainly to anyone who has been in the Merchant Navy – was penicillin. It had a massive effect on medicine that echoed down the centuries. The greatest benefit was that doctors could now get their patients out of their surgeries in record time – all by writing up a prescription for antibiotics. Even if the patient came in with a saucepan stuck on their head – out it was with the magic pills.

GOING LOCOMOTIVE

Scotland's heavy industries were ideal for making the giant metal machines we call locomotives and other people call trains. When first made there was great joy, coupled with confusion. What was to be done with them? It was at this point that someone thought they should invent railway tracks – which they did – and before long the whole country was criss-crossed with them. People in Glasgow could get on a train and within fifty minutes be wondering if the driver was going to shake off his hangover and turn up to take them out of the station. The economy received an unexpected boost as fish were taken by train to restaurants in England, however, the other passengers complained about them putting their fins up on the seats opposite.

These railways needed to cross rivers and, when they discovered these coal-fired engines were being snuffed out in the water, they thought it wise to build some bridges. It really was trial and error in those days. One such bridge crossed the River Tay and, showing the creativity that was the benchmark of Scottish invention, it was called the Tay Rail Bridge. Many were against the very idea. Dundonians feared that residents of Tayport and Newport would come and look down their noses at them, while residents of Tayport and Newport feared Dundonians would come over and look up their noses.

In Eighteen Oatcake, however, an even bigger disaster than the building of the bridge took place: the destruction of the bridge. The Tay Rail Bridge Disaster (again, creatively named) resulted in a lot of deaths. It was cruelly said by some* that they preferred a watery grave to a night out in Dundee, but that is just mean and way 'too soon', as comedians say to explain a distasteful joke that is made 'too soon'.

On a dark night a few days before Hogmanay (Hogmanay), the bridge gave way in strong winds. The watchman at the south of the bridge saw enormous sparks as the driver hit the brakes attempting to stop. So at least someone there saw fireworks at New Year. Too soon?

The disaster is now chiefly remembered through a poem so-bad-it's-terrible by the Dundee Bard (so named because he was 'barred' from entering any place containing a pen and paper), William McGonagall. McGonagall had a good conceit of himself and thought he was a poet and the unfortunate world didn't know it. He was trite, and always attempting to write. There, poetry is not so hard. Even if you're not called a bard.

* The residents of Tayport and Newport.

Many people now wish McGonagall himself was on that fateful train. But that would be mean. And definitely too soon.

FIRST FORTH BRIDGE

The Victorians now had the taste for building big things designed to sustain heavy loads: bridges, viaducts and the queen's corsets being three of them. One of their most famous projects was the Forth Bridge. Now there can be some confusion over this, as it was the first. The second Forth Bridge is also the Forth Bridge. There is now a third Forth Bridge but it won't be a Forth Bridge – it's the Queensferry Crossing.*

Now, the newfangled Queensferry Crossing sounds a bit like an Alistair MacLean novel featuring Cold War spies in a snowy Alpine pass looking to receive a Russian double agent. (I'm getting carried away with myself, it's just a big road bridge where drivers can queue and mutter and look at their dashboard clocks with alarm as they face another late arrival at the office.)

But back to the First Forth Bridge. When it was opened, many of the locals assumed the train would ride up and down the humps of the bridge. Sadly for them and generations of thrill seekers, the train didn't do this, it settled for going along on the flat. According to local

* This section might be funnier if listened to rather than read, so the upcoming audio book is heartily recommended.

legend, the painting of the bridge is never completed. The contractors are not stupid and know a bright red gravy train bridge when they see one.

GLASGOW

One city that grew during the Industrial Revolution was Glasgow. It became known as the workshop of the world, i.e. the place where tobacco is smoked by men in cardigans and adult magazines are carefully stored away. It had jobs and people wanted jobs, or rather they didn't want to be starving, and so they flocked to get these jobs. Unfortunately, this rapid growth in the populace resulted in diseases being common, although many people were too tired to get sick. By Nineteen Oatcake there were three-quarters of a million people living in Glasgow. Those dying to make room for the others weren't doing it in big enough numbers and conditions were not great. Many lived in slums in bad areas or, as estate agents of the time called them, 'up-and-coming areas'.

Folk lived in large buildings called 'tenements' and part of the routine of living in them was the communal cleaning of the stairs. Residents would take a turn in washing these stairs and those who didn't were called 'manky' (manky) or 'clarty' (clarty). The rats who also lived close by were called other things. The city was covered in a dense smoky fug, not all of it caused by wee men standing outside drinking establishments talking about horse racing. Everything got dirty. Laundrettes sprang up, using soap powders that advertised themselves as 'Getting those black clothes back to grey'. One good thing about the smog was that it prevented many from seeing how poor they were.

Eventually the municipal authorities decided that living in squalor was not good for the city's image and so the tenements were knocked down. Someone had thought to move the residents out first, which saved countless lives. New flats were built in large multi-storey buildings away from where the residents used to live. People being people, they soon became nostalgic for being called 'manky' or 'clarty' and wanted their slums back, thus proving that there is, indeed, no pleasing some people.

It is said that what keeps Glaswegians going is a lasting pride in their city. That, and a fervent dislike of Edinburgh. To move to Edinburgh is tantamount to declaring oneself a crazy person. Few do it. People in Edinburgh have heard of Glasgow but don't venture near, frightened they might end up manky or clarty.

REVOLTING WORKERS

We all know hardship at work. In one of the previous jobs held by the writer of this book, the coffee machine was on a different floor to his office. But he just got on with it. Not all workers are willing to put up with issues. Some rise up and demand change. They want more money, shorter hours, and a smaller chance of dying. And when do they want it? While they're still alive!

Others wanted a vote. Politicians were not keen, as there was a worry these voters might elect someone who was a socialist or a werewolf, or some other mystical and dangerous creature. The powers-that-were back then grudgingly granted men the vote as long as they owned a house with its own flaxen mill and sported whiskers. The masses thought this very acceptable and spent the rest of their lives glad in the knowledge that their country was being run by such a fair and equitable system.

Women wanted a vote, but their protests were not heard. The men were laughing too much and had sucked their whiskers into their own mouths, and were left crawling on the floor in hysterical amusement at the very idea of a lady voting. Honestly, whatever next? Chimneys without boys stuck up them? The women were not finished, however, and they plotted their next move while they cut the groins out of any male's trousers within reach.

UNIONS

Around this time, groups of workers grouped together in what were known as trade unions or, to some, *trades* unions. There were many disagreements, and even to this day no one quite knows what is correct. Some of these trade/trades unions were later amalgamated, but only the ones who had fillings put in by dentists. The unions were organised and if things weren't going well they'd arrange strikes which saw them stop work to hang around the factory gates rubbing their hands at a fire brazier. In summer, they would sweat more than when working, but it had to be done.

YON'S ENTERTAINMENT

Eventually, working conditions were relaxed as bosses realised it might lead to higher productivity if their workforce wasn't dead. Thousands of workmen and workwomen now found themselves with spare time.

One of the great leisure pastimes of Glasgow people was talking about going 'doon the watter'. Day trips were organised in which tens of thousands would get on board boats that would then sail down the River Clyde to coastal venues. This going 'doon the watter' lasted a day, but ensuing chat about how cold the tea was, how small the scones were, etc., could last *months.*

Entertainment was also provided to people in the form of live shows. Music halls and theatres would be filled with people keen to have a laugh, or maybe several. For a few shilling ha'penny bobs, you could see legendary figures such as Harry Lauder, who played a financially astute Scotsperson who sang songs and told funny wee stories. They say things are dumbed down now, but this guy was a megastar. Winston Churchill called him Scotland's greatest ambassador. That showed Winnie really should have cut down on the fun juice. Lauder was honoured by his birthplace, Portobello in Edinburgh, which named a road running past a railway yard after him.

IT'S GOING HOME

Another pastime was the great game of fitba' (fitba'), which had been played in the medieval era but was not the silky game of football we now know in Scotland. Scots who travelled abroad to countries like Brazil and loads of other countries took the game with them and the locals picked it up. You'd think the Brazilians would show some gratitude to the instigators of their beautiful game, but in 1982 they did the opposite, beating Scotland 4–1 in a game that proved you don't have to be an athlete to play in goal for a professional football side.

For the punters, football provided a perfect leisure time opportunity:

1. Fixed length games (ninety minutes, extra if the players got injured)
2. Easy access (every town had a football club, some more than one)
3. Opportunity to swear (for ninety minutes, more if the players were injured).

It's not surprising that it caught on, and great teams emerged such as Celtic, Rangers, Hibs, Hearts, Aberdeen, Dundee United, Dundee – and Partick Thistle emerged too.

One of the most unsavoury aspects was not just the greasy food that was served at games but the underlying animosity. There can be no discussion of football's emergence in Scotland without touching on the dark heart that lay beneath the thick woollen jerseys. Two teams in particular didn't like each other, but for legal reasons we are unable to name Rangers and Celtic. Fans of other teams couldn't believe the antipathy each held for the other. Why weren't they fighting the common enemy: the caterers?

HILLWALKING

Another leisure pursuit that arose was one that had previously been thought of as being daft. Scotland's hills and mountains have provided a rugged and inspiring landscape for painters, writers and calendar makers for many years. Locals and visitors alike have stood in awe of their majestic grandeur. Eventually it was thought an idea to go up these mountains, but as helicopters hadn't been invented yet this was pooh-poohed. Then a few brave souls stuffed some Kendal mint cake in their pockets, filled up a flask of Scotch broth and, making sure they had on their warmest kilts, headed upwards. After ten minutes, they stopped and breathed in deeply, and breathed in deeply some more, and tried to stop their hearts leaping out of their chest cavities. This uphill walking malarkey was no (mint) cakewalk! It was hard. The views were tremendous, though. From their vantage point they could see mile after mile of other hills and acres of heather and some sheep.

Eventually they got bored and headed on further up until they reached the top. These early 'hill trudgers'* surveyed the scene. All around they could see … nothing.

* The name was later changed to give it a more attractive vibe.

It was cloudy. Eventually it cleared and they could now see the stunning vistas of the hills and heather and sheep from earlier, but now from further up. After standing around for a bit, wishing they'd brought more mint cake, they headed back down. Chatting to fill some time, they discussed how great an experience it was and how it'd be great to do some more someday. If only there was a way to make it competitive …

Luckily for them, a Scotsperson invented 'Munros', which were mountains over 3,000ft in height (it was quite a job getting the tape measure straight). These Munros could now be 'bagged'. This meant that not only could people go up these mountains, they could tell everyone else about it and race to complete them before their pals.

18 THE NINETEENTH CENTURY OATCAKE

OR

GREAT WALTER SCOTT (AND OTHERS!)

A great Scot around this time was Walter Scott. He was a man of letters and knew them all, lower case *and* capitals, and boy could he use them. Scott's novel *Waverley*, about Edinburgh's train station, was a huge hit, along with *Kidnapped* which – spoiler alert! – is about a kidnapping.

Scott has been much criticised for creating a romanticised vision of the Highlands, but if you've ever spent a wet weekend in Fort William you'll take all the romanticising you can get. He is credited with inventing tourism in Scotland, so every time you are stuck behind a caravan on the road to Applecross you know who to blame.* For this achievement, the burghers of Edinburgh built a statue to commemorate the profits from rocketing hotel prices each summer during the Festival. You can still see the Scott Monument by going along Princes St and looking at it.

Amongst his many other achievements, Scott found the Scottish Crown Jewels in Edinburgh Castle. The Sceptre, Sword of State and Crown had lain undiscovered for years until being found by him in an unknown location in the castle called 'The Crown Room'.**

Sadly, the great Scott died after attempting to get himself out of bankruptcy by copious and frenetic writing. He would have tried scratch cards, but, despite them being invented a few pages ago, their invention hadn't reached the Borders yet.

* Yup, it's Walter.

** This is actually true. How quick on the uptake were these Victorian sleuths?

GEORGE FOUR

In Eighteen Oatcake the whole of Edinburgh trembled with excitement. Not with the imminent arrival of a new line of tweed underpants at Jenners department store, but something almost as exciting. A king was coming! The *Edinburgh Evening News* dropped its normal headline story of how terrible the pavements were to go big on this bombshell. The city went crazy for this king fellow. They had never seen a German before.

The celebrations were organised by Walter Scott, who convinced der Koenig to wear a kilt. The king went for the whole nineteen yards – literally – covering his large self in bright red plaid supplemented by pink-coloured tights so no one could see the royal legs in their brazen nudity. His attire was related to traditional Highland apparel as much as this book is to Scottish history, but it caught on. Eventually everyone, from entertainers such as Harry Lauder and Jack McConnell, could be seen baring their legs while sporting a comedic kilt. Highlanders laughed at the crazy vicissitudes of life – from being persecuted for their clothes one century, to being lauded and imitated the next. 'Ho ho!' they went, through gritted teeth.

GREYFRIARS BOBBY

In Eighteen Seventy Oatcake, the city of Edinburgh was rocked by sad news: a dog had died. But not just any dog. This was Greyfriars Bobby. Bobby had become attached, emotionally and physically by a lead, to his master.

When the master died, Bobby thought he was playing a big old joke and so hung around. Bobby wasn't too quick on the uptake and even when his master was put in a box, laid in the ground and covered with earth, he still thought the old boy would appear, saying, 'Gotcha, Bobby, you should see your face.' But he didn't appear and Bobby never saw his master's face or heard his voice again.

Bobby felt silly with all the time hanging around the graveyard, so decided to turn it into an art performance piece. Tourists and locals alike would stand engrossed as the little dog sat staring into space for hours on end. His static, tranquil stance became a symbol of complete devotion.

One day, little Bobby seemed more static and devoted than previously and when touched was found to be cold. He had died a week before but no one had noticed. Still waiting for his master, despite being dead? What a devoted little dog that Bobby was! A statue was made near to the cemetery and tourists can rub its nose for luck, although what is lucky about it is hard to detect. Lucky for the council worker employed to paint the little tyke's bronze nose – a job for life.

DAVID LIVINGSTONE'S GONE

David Livingstone was another great Scot around this time. Davie was a man of faith. He had to be, because by the end he had very little else left. Disease had taken its toll, as well as a lion which bit his arm forcing a very, very, very small tear to appear in this stoical Scot's eye. He didn't cry, though, oh no – it was African dust and he didn't even wince when the doctor managed to pour vinegar, paprika and chilli powder into the wound, as was the custom then for treating large feline bites. All this before the outpatient treatment of fire ants were marched up to eat any of the pus-filled bits.

In one of history's most renowned events, Livingstone famously met Henry Stanley, the great American reporter, who was from Wales. When Stanley first shook hands with our David, he said, 'Dr Livingstone, I presume you've received my letters, telegrams and missives and are just blanking me?'

Livingstone was a missionary on a mission who travelled the African continent looking for the source of the Nile. Sadly, he didn't find it and failed to meet one of his Key Performance Indicators. He was sent on a team-building away day, despite his protests that every day for him was an away day.

Eventually and sadly, he died. His heart was buried under a tree and every day a lion would come and sit beside it, waiting on Livingstone to return, until someone told the beast that this sort of thing had already been done in Edinburgh by a dog.

THE ONE O'CLOCK GUN

Many towns and cities are festooned with large clocks. London has Big Ben and there are definitely others. Edinburgh wasn't going to take this lying down. It was going to tell the time by firing an artillery gun from its castle ramparts. Every day at exactly one o'clock p.m. the city would reverberate as the gun was set off. As well as providing residents with an audible reminder of the time, it would give unsuspecting tourists a reason to visit Jenners* to buy new underpants, tweed or otherwise.

THE WEE FREES

The Wee Frees is a nickname for the Free Church of Scotland, which broke away from the Church of Scotland following a dispute over whether there should be a comma between 'Onward' and 'Christian Soldiers'. The Wee Frees formed their own God-worshipping group and took their name from a Christmas carol. Their main tenet was not liking anything apart from God and plain living. On a Sunday, they banned working, cleaning, watching TV, drinking and sudoku. You weren't even allowed to sing. As the old Scottish proverb has it, 'Sing is only one letter away from sin'.

QUEEN VIC

Big Queen Vic, as no one called her within earshot, was a regular visitor to Scotland. It was rumoured that part of the attraction was not just the rugged Highland landscapes and the babbling brooks brim-full of fish, but a certain John Brown. Brown was a member of staff and was very 'close' to the queen. In one scandalous photograph, he can be seen 'holding the queen's reins'. Heavens to Betsy!

* Other shops selling underpants are available.

Women of Society keeled over in shock at the sheer effrontery, but when they were told it was a method of holding a horse they refused to countenance the thought of a common man so close to the monarch's saddle.

Big Vicky loved to be driven around in a carriage as walking wasn't the done thing for royalty around this time, but despite avoiding any risk of falling, tripping or being a bit out of breath she did eventually die. She gave her name to a medal, a park, an era and a sponge cake, and that is something her Georgian descendants could only dream of.

19 THE NOT-SO-GREAT WORLD WAR

OR

THE MUD AND BEING SHELLED NOVELTY IS WEARING OFF

We've all seen it: a domestic argument spills onto the street, the neighbours get involved and before you know it, 17 million people have died.

The First World War – they were confident of a sequel – began in Nineteen Oatcake and ended once enough people had been killed. It wasn't all doom and gloom, however, as some of the soldiers managed to get book deals, particularly in poetry, which had none of the connotations of being produced by publicly funded workshy layabouts it does now. Writing poems about war wasn't easy, as there are few words rhyming with artillery, howitzer and argghh!

In the Not-So-Great War, Scots troops were, of course, present in large numbers. Hey, it was the chance of causing some chaos on a large scale. At the start they were excited, keen to have a go at the English again. When they heard it was Germany, their faces fell a bit but perked up when told they could have a sly kick at any Englishmen they passed on their way to the trenches.

This was no rammy on the seafront at Saltcoats, though. Some of the soldiers had a look at the mud, the filth, smelt the stench of death and thought, 'Nah, changed my mind, I'll just nip home.' When the small print was pointed out to them, they just laughed, saying, 'Oh what are we like?', and happily got on with it, before they were shot by their own side for not being prepared to be shot by the other side. War is not just hell, it is profoundly stupid.

Life in the trenches was bad. To give some idea, you know when you get to your bus stop just in time to see the bus sailing past five minutes earlier than its scheduled departure time? It's just like that. Yup, it's bad. Scots troops were able to prevent their trousers from getting wet in the mud by not wearing them. They were frightening the other troops – especially the Germans – who asked politely if they wouldn't mind putting something else on. The Scots troops had packed this national item of clothing as they'd been told they were being sent to be kilted. Unfortunately, they'd misheard.

In the first winter of the war there was a celebrated Christmas Truce. It wasn't celebrated by all of the Scots in the front line, who said they were having nothing whatsoever to do with it.* And they didn't, passing the traditional festive day by muttering under their breath about 'bloody Christmas' and complaining that Christmas wasn't a time for peace.

There was some bad feeling amongst those who had exchanged gifts with the Germans, when they refused to accept returns on Boxing Day as the recipients didn't have a receipt. This undoubtedly led to ill-feeling that contributed to the war not finishing by Christmas that year. Or the year after that. Or the one after that. Or even the one that followed that one.

It was only when the Germans finally agreed that vouchers would be issued for unwanted items that the war could finally end.

* This is actually true.

20 THE INTER-WAR YEARS

OR

BUDDY, CAN YOU SPARE ME A SHILLING?

Men came back from the front to find that women had taken their jobs. 'Yass!' many cried, glad to be rid of them, but some of the women were happy to hand these boring jobs back to the menfolk.

Many women had made a good living and thought it was time for men and women to be equal. They also wanted to take part in the democratic process, to have the same rights as men to spoil their ballot papers by drawing a small cat or a picture of a train. Women campaigners were called Suffragettes because they wanted to have suffrage.* They had banners made which had the words 'Deeds not words' on them. When it was pointed out by smart-arsed men that this was ironic, they soon felt the full weight of an Edwardian lady boot being placed firmly in their own ballot box. Around this time, there were other protests too, which were, of course, to echo down the centuries.

RED CLYDESIDE

After the war there were plenty of tanks lying about and, rather than see them rusting, the government of the day thought they'd be great for other uses: opening garden fêtes, carrying the mail, or chasing protesting workers down Glasgow streets. It all came about because people in that city weren't happy. They were mad as hell and weren't going to take it any more, so they rose up and protested. They marched into George Square and shouted and made

* In the same way those protesting for decent kitchens were called Kitchenettes.

speeches and shouted about the speeches and shouted while giving the speeches (public address systems hadn't been invented by a Scotsperson yet).

Now this wasn't appreciated by Those In Power, who were trying to sleep and who also wanted to keep things as they were, thank you very much. 'We'll see about that,' said the Protestors.

'Oh yeah?' replied Those In Power.

'Oh yeah!' came back the Protestors.

'Yeah?'

'Yeah!'

This exchange of Wildean wit was interrupted by those aforementioned tanks coming into the discussion and ending it.

JOHN MACLEAN

John Maclean was a prominent member of the Red Clydeside movement. He wished for people to have better lives and not be so poor all the time. Well, this utter madness wasn't going to get far, was it? Maclean was imprisoned for his beliefs and also for his buzz-cut haircut that said, 'Are you looking at my pit bull?'

Maclean was given special treatment while in the jail. Every night guards would torment him by saying, 'Maclean?', to which the prisoner would have to reply, 'Yes, I had a bath this morning.' If he failed to answer he would be given a warm bath with capitalist bath salts and a free-market loofah. But worse was to come for Maclean. He was force-fed food – a practice that causes revulsion and incredulity as:

1. No one in Scotland has to be encouraged to eat
2. Maclean wasn't actually on hunger strike.

His supporters were appalled and aggrieved, and some were alliteratively angry also. They thought that the prison authorities were trying to fatten him up in order to taunt him with cries of 'Fatso', 'Chubber' and 'Fatty Boom-Boom Big Pants'.

Maclean was eventually released from prison, but died aged 44, disappointed that his age was not made into a bingo call.

STRIKE!

Around this time, the country ground to a halt (not literally, it still rotated along with the other constituent parts of the planet Earth) as General Strike ordered his troops to shoot anyone in a trades/trade union (industrial dispute resolution was still at a rudimentary stage). Fortunately, he was persuaded not to shoot everyone, as this would mean there was no one to pour his whiskies.

The strikers wanted a reduction in their working hours and an increase in wages. Some got confused and wanted more working hours and an increase in wage cuts. The fat-cat bosses readily accepted this demand, much to the chagrin of workers, who had never used that word before.

The miners who had struck to get less working hours now had to work eight hours a day instead of seven, but they accepted this reverse with a cheery grin and returned to work, whistling as they went with their flat caps at a jaunty angle. Decades later, this would be resolved by them all having no hours to work – but more of that later.

CULTURE AND THAT

At times, culture in Scotland is viewed the same way as removing a splinter with a hot needle: we know it's good for us but we don't enjoy others doing it to us. In the Nineteen Twenty Oatcakes a flowering of creative talent took place that gained the name 'The Scottish Renaissance'. This reboot of culture had amongst its many talents that of a poet – and by God did he let us know it – known as Hugh MacDiarmid. He was famous for his epic work, *A Drunk Man Looks at 18 Months For Public Urination*, which was too clever and wordy for many to understand. (Of course, the writer of this book got *all* its literary allusions but space prevents too detailed a critique.)

Hugh was a proponent of a Scots language called Lallans. Its name derives from the sound people made when sticking their fingers in their ears when one of his poems were read out. MacDiarmid was joined in renaissanceing the crap out of Scotland by figures such as 'Storming' Norman MacCaig and William 'Soapy' Soutar. Soutar wrote a poem on his deathbed, but luckily it was in permanent marker and once out of the laundry was able to be published. MacCaig wrote a series of poems called *A Man in Assynt*, which was followed by *Another Man in Assynt*, which was then followed by *A Civil Partnership in Assynt*.

Gaelic poetry (which is hard because little rhymes with 'microwave') was represented by Sorely 'Tested' MacLean. Sorely was a great talent, or at least that's what those who speak Gaelic say. And we have to take their *facal* for it.

But it wasn't just poetry that was written. Books – many without pictures – were published in this burgeoning of the culture. Lewis 'Classic' Gibbon's *Sunset Song* was acclaimed by those who read it, and also by those who didn't but wanted to feel part of something. Its lyrical and yet gritty depiction of simple yet complex farming folk of the north-east yet south-west was destined to be remembered down the centuries.

It's very easy to forget the contribution of women to the Renaissance, but luckily this author didn't, just in time. Women wrote some great books around this time. Dame 'Muriel' Spark (who was a woman) wrote what is commonly accepted to be the best novel about a snooty girls' school in Morningside: *The Prim Miss Jean Brodie*. She went on to write other books, each with a different title.

Although nothing to do with this flowering of talent, but a writer all the same,* Arthur 'Conan' Doyle had invented the character we know as Sherlock Holmes. Looking at the sales figures, many later Scottish writers turned to crime. They wrote many, many, many novels featuring authority-opposing and maverick sleuths who solved crimes their own way. There was Laidlaw, Rebus and there were definitely many others.

* And also just remembered.

ART ATTACK

Now a country that had the Forth Rail Bridge would always produce painters. The Scottish Colourists were well regarded – they never went over the lines – and would spend days doing tasteful studies of nudes, and minutes doing the still lives and landscapes that brought in the money.

Another group of talented artists was known as the Glasgow Boys. They were similar to another group called the Glasgow Girls in that they had Glasgow in their name. The Glasgow Boys went on to become the Glasgow Men, then the Glasgow Men Who Worry About How Often They Get Up In The Night For A Pee. Their work echoes down the centuries for anyone who can remember a single painting they did.

One of the figures around this time was, of course, Charles 'Rennie' Mackintosh, who was an architect, an artist, a husband and a moustache wearer. He designed the famous art school in Glasgow which has produced some fantastically gifted artists, including the man who played the big hairy fella in the Harry Potter films.

TV STAR

In Ninety Twenty Oatcake, a Scotsperson displayed an invention that would change the world. On a flickering screen the faint images of celebrities dancing with horses on an ice rink could be seen. This revolution in home entertainment ushered in countless educational and worthwhile programmes. And stuff made by STV too.

Television would see the end of families standing around a piano, or sitting together knitting and talking to each other.

Thank God.

THE GREAT DEPRESSING

Contrary to common myth and fable, the Great Depressing is not named after dents left in car roofs by Wall Street bankers after they found they were no longer filthy rich. The effect of this financial calamity rippled around the world. It even reached Scotland, where shipyards and locomotive factories were closed and the doors locked up. Workers banged on these doors until they were let out. Many then got on their bikes and cycled away to be unemployed in other places. Others got on the ships they had built and sailed to foreign lands such as Canada, America and Arran.

But there was only one way to get everybody back working properly again. You got it – a war!

21 THE SECOND NOT-SO-GREAT WORLD WAR

OR

WHO DO YOU THINK YOU'RE KILLING, MR HITLER?

The decade* of the Nineteen Thirty Oatcakes saw the advent of fascism, where people marched about and picked on minorities. The aristocracy were perplexed: could you wear a black shirt with a tuxedo? Was the armband worn at dinner tables or only in the lounge?

One of the major fascists around this time was Adolf Hitler. He'd won *Austria's Got Fascists* and *The Swastika Factor*, before reaching the top. He was unbalanced, purportedly having only one manball, and this made him dislike pretty much everyone in the world. He did like Nazis, however, and also Eva Braun, whom he eventually married. For his honeymoon he arranged a surprise for his new bride: cyanide. Realising he couldn't live without her and wishing to avoid writing thank-you letters for the wedding gifts, he shot himself. All good things come to an end. And very bad ones too.

WAR

Having made an enormous arse of the first one, the powers-that-were decided to try again, but the Second World War was just as bad and for some (i.e. those that didn't make it to the street parties on account of being dead) it was much, much worse. There is a strain of thought that the sequel is never as good as the original, but WW2 went beyond its predecessor: millions of deaths, untold heartbreak, global misery and destruction.

* Not all decades run for ten years. The Nineteen Eighty Oatcakes are often reduced to six years on fashion grounds.

However, on the other hand, there were some plus points. Great films were made featuring the war. And while the Luftwaffe bombing was clearly A Bad Thing, when raids hit warehouses containing Harry Lauder records, well, then you know, perhaps it wasn't as black and white as maybe first thought?

HESS DROPS IN

One day in Nineteen Forty Oatcake, Scots awoke to astonishing news: a tourist had come! Unfortunately, it was in the form of senior Nazi Rudolf Hess. Hess was a big pal of Hitler and had flown all the way from Germany for what turned into a long-duration city break. The traditional Scottish hospitality was duly extended and we just would not let him go, and he was jailed until he died. Many conspiracy theories have grown up over the years about exactly why Herr Hess came to Scotland, and the one that he wanted to buy a kilt in the Hess tartan cannot be confirmed nor denied.

MERRY AUGUST (WAR IS OVER)

Scots fought wherever they could: France, Italy, Burma, the deserts of North Africa and the pubs of North London. Peace was eventually restored after the biggest bangs anyone had ever heard. The Americans showed they had the biggest bombs in town and, unfortunately for those living in Hiroshima and Nagasaki, it was their towns.

POST-WAR

OR

I'M SO OVER THIS RATIONING

Despite the war being over, there was to be no respite from fear and anxiety as in Nineteen Forty Oatcake the Edinburgh Festival started. At first it was just a small thing and no one was too worried. After all, who would want to come to this cold, windy city in the north of Britain to sit in small rooms being charged a fortune to listen to a comedian talking about problems with Putney taxi drivers?

There was nervousness from the local Edinburghers, who weren't sure they'd be able to get away with charging so much for hotel rooms, but they persevered and eventually their enthusiasm for the arts (of making money) paid off. For some there was to be no compensation, and citizens would hide in their attics for the month of August until there was no fear of being offered a flyer for a show on the Royal Mile about a depressed donkey with a God complex.*

HOLIDAYS

In Nineteen Fifty Oatcake an event took place that shocked and appalled many Scots: Christmas was made a public holiday. What an affront to common decency, expecting people to work for nothing on the day celebrating the birth of Jesus! When they were told it was a *paid* holiday, they were even more upset. What kind of tribute was *that* to the originator of their religion, sitting at home eating and drinking to their jollification and receiving money for it? There was no pleasing some people, but most got used

* That actually sounds good.

to the idea quickly, especially when Morecambe and Wise were invented to fill the gap of families sitting sullenly looking at each other over the boiled sprouts, daring one of them to touch that Harry Lauder record.

YON'S MORE ENTERTAINMENT

Scotland can reduce people to hysterics, sometimes intentionally. It has a rich heritage in producing funny people such as Billy Connolly, Chic Murray, Kevin Bridges and the person who devised Edinburgh's Tram project. While comedy can produce laughs, another arena provides even more opportunities for a good belly laugh.

POLITICS

In Nineteen Forty Oatcake tremors were felt in the political landscape as the Scottish National Party (Scottish National Party) made a monumental leap onto the political springboard, bounced onto the trampoline of national prominence and landed on the **<insert other gymnastic analogy here before going to print>** when they had a Member of Parliament elected. An SNP MP! No one hadda thunk it possible.

The party had formed earlier, as it hadn't existed before. Its aims were clear: to have a political party called the Scottish National Party. Once this was achieved, the members relaxed. Job done. Then, after a few years of sitting about twiddling thumbs, finishing sudokus, etc., a few bolder ones felt they should go further and have some policies.

A break-out workshop session was duly arranged which came back with large sheets of flip-chart paper covered with ideas. One caught the eye and became law: no more break-out sessions. Another made an impact: Home Rule.

The members demanded Home Rule without knowing what it really meant. Whose home? They decided *all* the homes in the whole country were to be ruled differently from homes in another country (for example, England). This intrigued the electorate for years, with many wondering if it would lead to war with England. Some strained their finger muscles crossing them so much.

WAR WITH ENGLAND

There wasn't really a war with England in the Nineteen Fifty Oatcakes, but there was a stramash (stramash). When the people of Westminster woke up one Boxing Day feeling something was missing they were right to do so, as Scottish tourists had come home from their abbey with a 'souvenir'. This wasn't a fridge magnet or a double-decker-shaped pencil sharpener either. It was the Stone of Destiny! Cue uproar! The famous Stone had been removed from under the arses of future queens and kings of the land. Where was it? Those who had taken it knew, but they weren't for telling. Eventually the stone was returned and sent back to London, where a royal behind duly sat on it in Nineteen Fifty Oatcake in front of millions of television viewers. This wasn't a strange reality show called Monarchs Test Furniture, but the Coronation from which a chicken-based delicacy was invented by – do you have to ask?

THE KING

Elvis Presley lit up the Nineteen Fifty Oatcakes as The Beatles lit up the Nineteen Sixty Oatcakes, as Fran and Annie didn't do the following decade. Elvis, who was known as The King, despite coming from a deeply republican country, sang, danced and made women (and some men, who had to keep it very quiet back then) think thoughts that would have made Robert Burns blush. Elvis was like Burns in some ways: he had charm by the bucket load and he was talented by the bucket load, but he also ordered fried chicken by the bucket load. Yes, like Burns, he died young. You'd think, by the way Elvis gobbled down the junk food and then died of a heart attack, he was Scottish – and that's because he was. His ancestors came from the Auld Country. Did Scotland invent Rock 'n' Roll? That's not for the writer of this book to say.*

HOME RULE, PART 2

In Nineteen Sixty Oatcake, the Scottish National Party celebrated as their dreams had become reality: Home Rule had arrived. The Prime Minister of Great Britain was Sir Alec Douglas-Home. When the hung-over revellers realised this error, they cursed the demon drink even more. Some, however, said that it counted and they could now stop having to constantly campaign for it.

* Of course it did!

POWER

Scotland is blessed with boundless natural resources such as its scenery, wildlife and endless rain. Scotspersons have long wondered what to do with all this water. They could only turn so much of it into swally after all. Clever types at the Department of Clever Types came up with the idea of converting it to electricity. This hugely upset Christian alcoholics, who were hoping for a Jesus-style transformation into something a bit more 'grape-based'. However, this electricity would prove useful as Scots could now power up the television sets that they'd invented.

ANE SMALL STEP

In Nineteen Sixty Oatcake the world stood still, or sat if they'd bagged a seat in time, engrossed as a human walked on the moon for the first time. Those in Scotland were especially enraptured – STV cameras hadn't missed it.

The first man on the moon was, of course, a Scot: Neil Armstrong, who hailed from the Scottish county of Ohio. Neil spoke with an American accent but was definitely Scottish. When he put his foot on the lunar soil, as the first human to do so, he uttered words that would pass into legend and echo down the decades. Words the world would never forget: 'Buzz, we've got a braw day for it.'

GLITZ, GLAMOUR AND POWER CUTS

The Nineteen Seventy Oatcakes saw much grief and strife, with unrest, strikes and much moaning about the price of Spangles. People wanted more money and less work to do. 'This is outrageous,' said those who had more money and less work to do. So it went, backwards and forwards, until those in trades/trade unions went on strike and got no money *and* no work to do. This decade wasn't all hair and disco dancing.

Workers downed tools. Those who didn't use tools, such as lorry drivers, bought tools so they could then down them. This was good for the tool companies, and their workers kept quiet about that lovely overtime. Others who did well out of industrial action included the firms that made the metal braziers used by workers to stand around at factory gates. However, the real money was made by those who made the famous donkey jackets – *the* must-wear item for the striking season, available in black, black and also black.

As a result of the strikes, a three-day week was introduced by the government of the day.* Wednesday, Thursday and Friday were selected, leaving the other days very unhappy. Strikes were threatened – Monday was the ringleader in all of this – until it was pointed out you couldn't withdraw your labour if you weren't employed, so legal action was withdrawn and the full week was restored. 'Phew!' said calendar makers.

* Things were so changeable that you could have a different government the next day then the previous one back in by lunchtime the following day.

Around this time, the economy wasn't doing very well and much talk was made of the 'Balance of Payments'. Everyone agreed something should be done but, as no one really knew what it was, they would just nod when the subject came up without offering an opinion. A few years before, the Prime Minister of the Week (things were more stable then) had taken action and devalued the pound. He was going to unvalue it, or even sub-value it at one point, but went ahead with his crazy scheme that not many people properly understood.* He said there would be no change to the pound in your pocket. This showed a great lack of financial knowledge of the time: who the hell had a pound?!

The great heavy industries that had made Scotland untidy and very tired were diminishing around this time. The industrial heartlands were being deindustrialised in the way Clydebank had been dearchitectured by the Luftwaffe. It was not an easy time for those affected by not having a job, but some were to head north, to a place where a great discovery was about to be made.

OIL BE DAMNED

Around this time a great discovery was made. Lying under the North Sea, off the Scottish coast and deep under the ocean floor, lay untold wealth and fortune. Diamonds, rubies and emeralds – in the form of sludgy black oil – lay waiting. This 'North Sea Oil' was discovered in 'fields',

* Hello!

but initial efforts to recover it failed when the first tractor drivers 'drowned'. Boats were used thereafter and things started to take off, including the helicopters that took oil workers to their oil rigs.

These oil rigs were large metal structures that sat in the middle of the sea and had drilling equipment, sleeping quarters, dining facilities and toilets. Men would live on these for a couple of weeks and, although it seemed harsh, they were then sent to Aberdeen for two weeks afterwards. Huge amounts of revenue (money) was raised and invested wisely by the governments of the day.*

THE NINETEEN HATETIES

Grim times were had in the Nineteen Eighty Oatcakes. Future football pundit Alan Hansen caused a mix-up in defence that led the Soviet Union to score against Scotland in the Nineteen Eighty Oatcake World Cup. To many, this might appear a trivial aspect of a decade torn with strife. Thousands of people lost their jobs as communities reeled under the onslaught of a government that seemed to be determined to fight a class war. More importantly, why didn't he just let Willie Miller clear it on his own?

There was more grief and strife in the Nineteen Eighty Oatcakes with a horrible Englishwoman making life awful for those she regarded as mere animals to be ordered around. But not everyone watched Barbara

* Look around!

Woodhouse, as they were too busy burning effigies of M■■■■t T■■■■r.*

T■■■■r was much loved by those who called her mum, but everyone else thought she was pretty frightful. She reminded many of that dinner lady that would refuse to give you extra beans even though there was no one behind you in the queue and you were well known for loving beans, and she knew that you knew that the beans were going to be thrown out if no one ate them. That's who she was: a bean stealer.

At the start of the next decade she was ousted from power. T■■■■r was a driven woman, especially the day a car took her away from Downing Street. She famously was seen to cry, the onion in her top pocket working its magic as her tears melted their way through the car's floor and the tarmac underneath.

ENVIRONMENTAL ISSUES

Many terrible environmental events have taken place on Scotland's shores and soil: the *Braer* oil-tanker spillage in Shetland, the avian flu-ridden swan corpse in Fife, and Donald Trump's hair in Aberdeenshire. While the oil was dispersed and the swan taken away for burial, nothing could remove the image of that golden disaster so close to home. A whole wind farm was built to try to dislodge

* You can't say her name like him out of the Harry Potter films, you know the one? Voldemort, that's it. Oops.

this hairstyle, rumoured by many to be of extra-terrestrial origin, but to no avail. No one wants a nuclear explosion to ever take place in Scotland, but it might finally reveal the secrets of the rug. Luckily its wearer disappeared from public view and never caused any more upset.

CLONE WARS

Scotland, as has been demonstrated, has a rich history of invention. Determined to be included on the tea towels of great inventions, scientists at the Roslin Institute came up with a corker: they would clone a sheep. Some scoffed at the idea, saying, 'Why on Earth would you want to copy an animal known for its lack of individuality?' The scientists had a witty rejoinder, 'We cloned a sheep!' The world's very first living cloned sheep was revealed in Nineteen Ninety Oatcake. She was given the name 'Dolly', in honour of the renowned country and western singer, as the Roslin scientists worked strict office hours: 9 to 5.

IT'S BACK!

In Nineteen Ninety Oatcake, Scotland was given its own parliament and was told to look after it and not overfeed it. From now on, Scots could have their own political scandals and not have to travel to London to get caught out. They still got to go to London, though, to the parliament there. And the one in Europe.* And, of course, there were still

* For a while at any road.

the little council ones too. So, with all these governing bodies, everything was great and any issues were sorted out pretty smartly, as you'd expect with so many great minds working towards the common good.

This new Scottish Parliament needed new blood, and the length, breadth and height of Scotland was scoured for those willing to devote their lives for £50,000 a year plus expenses. Er, for the privilege of serving their public. Scotland did away with the notion of having a 'Prime Minister' and instead plumped for having a 'First Minister'. This clear distinction showed that Scotland was very much a distinct country that was going to govern in its own way and was in no way mimicking its larger and more southern counterpart.

Momentous days are rare, but one such day was the day Scotland's Parliament reopened for business. All over the country, citizens celebrated the change from being badly run by an out-of-touch administration in London to being badly run by an out-of-touch administration in Edinburgh. Chests almost burst with pride.

The work soon began for Scotland's MSPs (Members of Some Parliament). They had to fill in expenses forms, eat pies when supposedly in the debating chamber, go on trips gathering information unavailable on the Internet, and so on. It wasn't easy, but they got through it with skill and fortitude. And pies.

The parliament tackled the main issues of the day and, for the first time in 300 years, laws were passed in Scotland to change the way Scots lived. A new law meant that drinkers could now not smoke in a pub. Discontent was expected, but smokers were not in pubs to just smoke, they were there to drink and they weren't going to risk access to swally over a cigarette or two, no matter how utterly addictive those glorious thin white sticks of smoky yum were to them. Other laws were made, but no one can really remember them. There might have been one about dogs?

The parliament had its critics. James Ranaldson, Eric Maguire, Elizabeth Alness, Robin Donald, Flora Donald, Billy Matheson, Neil Austin, Sylvia McPherson, Fiona Oldman, Louise Parks, Claire Burns, Liz Thomson, Ida O'Neill, Jim Naylor, Ian Rawlinson, Dennis Tyndall, Sean Dibbs and Frank Morrison, to name just a few. Oh, and George MacInnes and Lisa Findlay were not huge fans. And Denise Oswald was hardly enamoured, come to think of it.

THE BUILDING

It was felt the nation needed a bold statement to symbolise Scottish rebirth and they certainly did that, by employing an architect from Spain. A main source of the criticism levelled at the parliament building was the cost: £400 million. £400,000,000. Four. Hundred. Million. Pounds. Fourhundredmillionpounds. No matter how many times you see it written down, it still doesn't get any smaller. The original estimate was £40 million. That's like going to buy a birthday card for a person about to be 8 and coming back with one saying 'You're 80!'

It had cost more than anyone imagined, even those paid to imagine exactly how much it would cost, but the construction companies – and their families as it neared

Christmas – could relax knowing that many pounds would be falling their way. Eventually it was opened and everyone could settle down to getting bored. This they did. However, this boredom was about to evaporate.

FREEDOM! OR NOT!

In Twenty Oatcake it was announced that the country – or rather the people in it – was to vote on whether they were to remain a part of the UK or become apart from the UK. Wild promises were made in the frenetic campaigning. If Scotland stayed it would get its own weather with a guaranteed two sunny weeks in July; the football team would get a bye to the final of the World Cup, and sports commentators would stop saying, 'That Scottish idiot Andy Murray has blown it again.'

Those on the other side had a cunning plan. Wind turbines would be built until every hill would be covered and if a Yes vote was delivered, Scotland would cast off and sail under its own power to the Mediterranean.

Polling day was a day that echoed down the centuries. A proud nation stood up and declared: No. Many voters had thought carefully, but the idea of all that foreign food and sunshine put them off.

Scotland.

THE END

ACKNOWLEDGEMENTS & AUTHOR'S NOTE

Thanks go to Chrissy McMorris, Alex Waite and all at The History Press without whom this book would not be in your hands. And thanks also to Alan Rowe for his great illustrations that bring some much-needed levity.

Special thanks go to my wife and family for allowing space and time to write such nonsense.

All opinions in this book are those of the author of this book and complaints should be addressed, but not sent. It's just a silly book.